CONTEMPORARY SAYINGS

21ST CENTURY HAND BOOK OF QUOTES

VOLUME-01

ANIL AGRAWAL

INDIA • SINGAPORE • MALAYSIA

ISBN 979-8-89610-726-2

This book is dedicated to

My Loving son

Samarth Agrawal *(Former Civil Judge)*

Contents

Man

"M*an's basic instinct,*
Is to doubt himself................
Rarely do people think good of
*themselves.***"** *!!!!!!!!!!!!*

"A *man is made of multiple faces,*
Life get wasted in deciphering a friendly
*face.***"** *!!!!!!!!!!*

"**A** *man who is putting you down*
Must necessarily be weak-willed,
Leave him,,,,,,,,,,,,
And proceed." !!!!!!!!!!!!!!!!!!!!!!!!!!

"**A***ttitudes are flexible,*
They are bendable, foldable.............
For a better social order,
People should always try to
accommodate." !!!!!!!!!!!

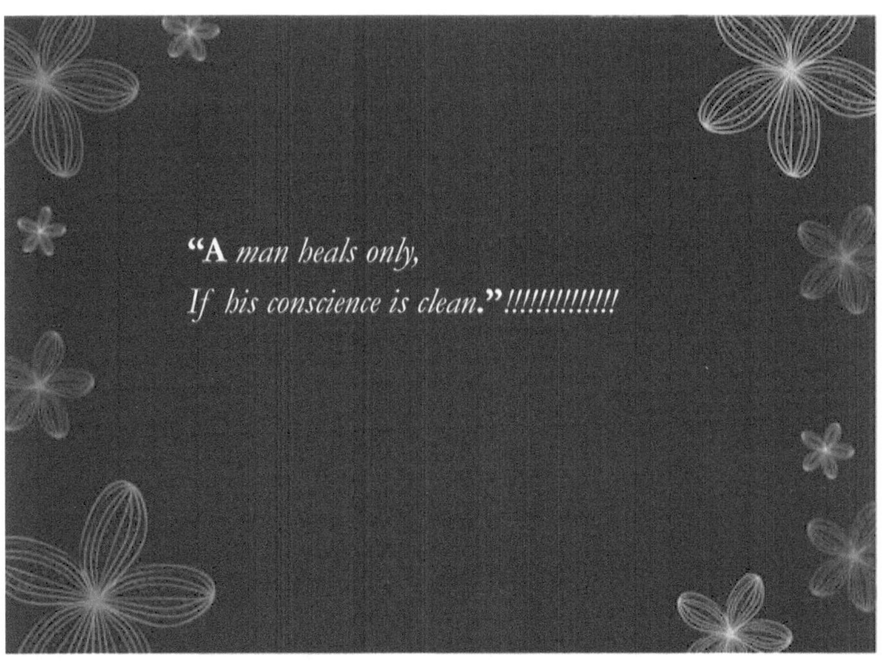
"A man heals only,
If his conscience is clean."!!!!!!!!!!!!!!

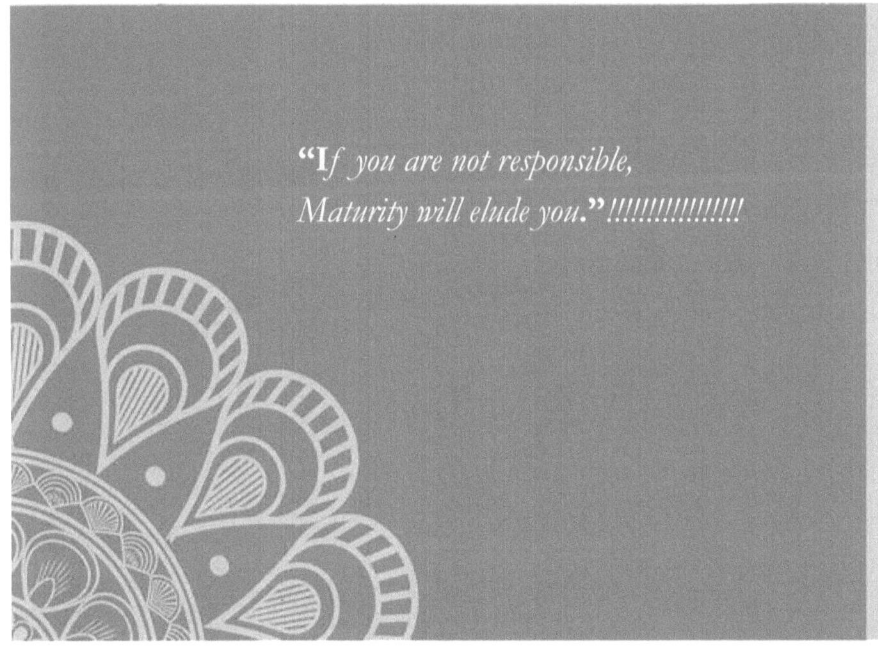
"If you are not responsible,
Maturity will elude you."!!!!!!!!!!!!!!!!!!

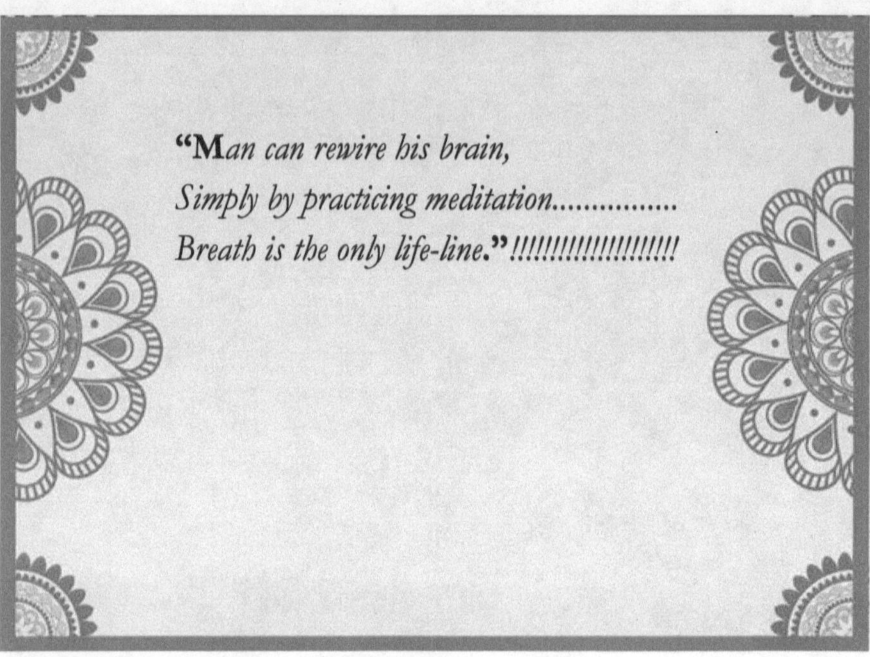
"Man can rewire his brain,
Simply by practicing meditation................
Breath is the only life-line."!!!!!!!!!!!!!!!!!!!!!!

"The foremost and primary
nature of man,
Is his reactionary
instinct."!!!!!!!!!!!!!!!!!

*"**N**ever judge a person with his abilities,*
Rather see to it whether he is empath and compassionate,
Invariably, under the cover of abilities people perpetrate injustices." !!!!!!!!!!!!!!!!!!!!!!!!!!!!!!!!!!!!

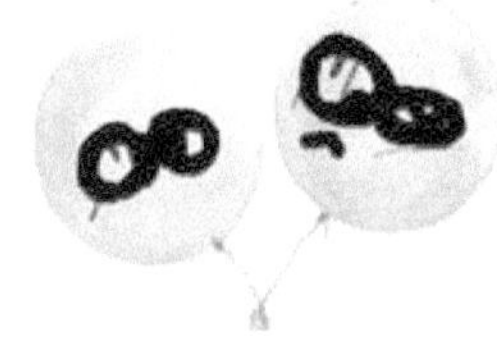

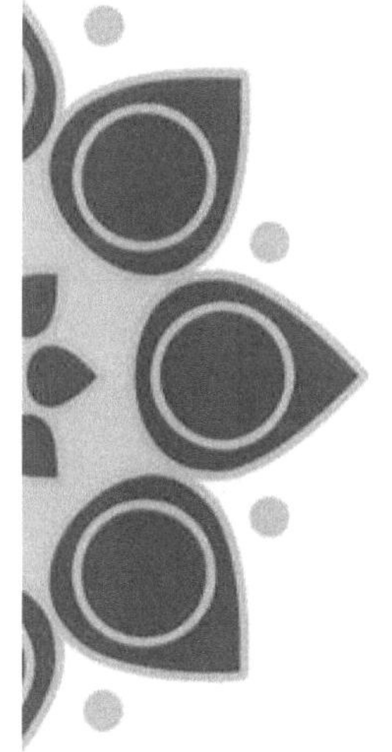

*"**T**he problem with man is!!!!!!!*
He only understands big wins,,,,,,,,,,
Always celebrate small wins for,
Small is beautiful,
Celebrating small wins shows your humil nature,
A man celebrating only big wins is somewhere down the line attitudinal." !!!!!!!!!!!!!!!!!!!!!!!!!!!

"**B***e a man of bending aspirations,*
You will never outstep."!!!!!!!!!!!!!!!!!!!!!!!!!

"A *worthy man never sees his worth,*
And this paradoxically is his great humil strength." !!!!!!!!!!

"A *man invents himself by,*
Becoming integral and empathyful." !!!!!!!!!!!!

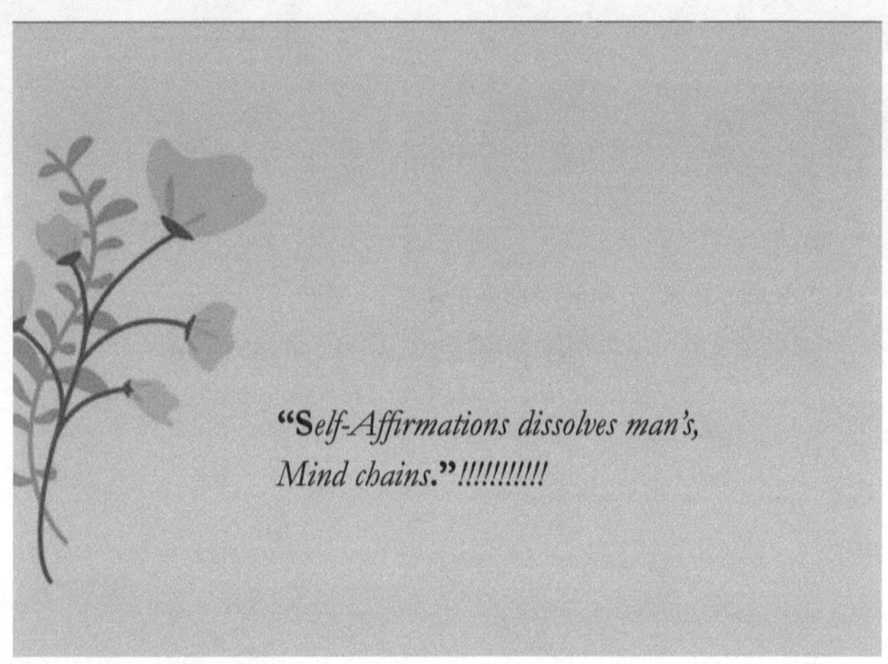
“**S***elf-Affirmations dissolves man’s,*
Mind chains.” !!!!!!!!!!!!

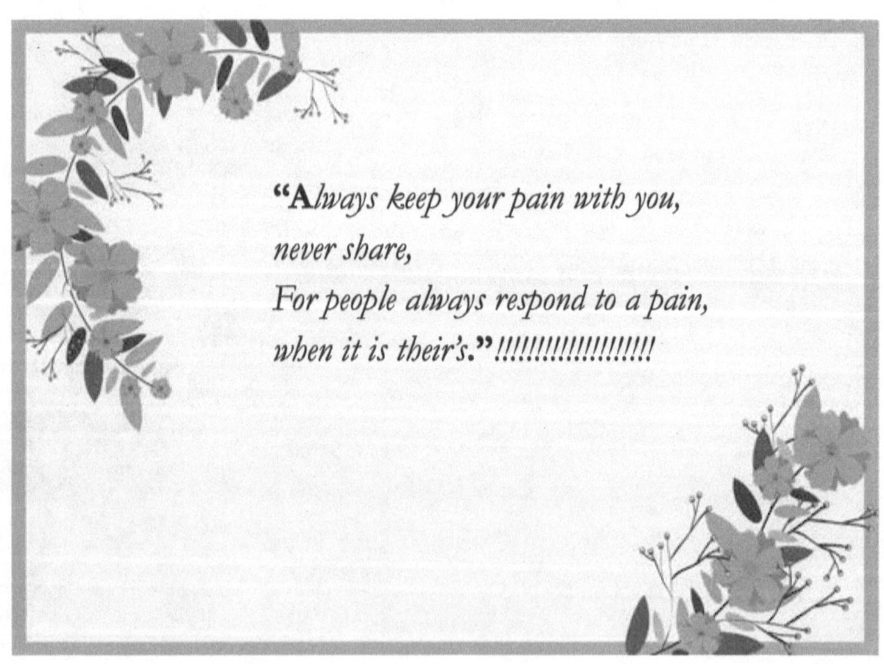
“**A***lways keep your pain with you,*
never share,
For people always respond to a pain,
when it is their’s.” !!!!!!!!!!!!!!!!!!!!

“**A** *bitter heart,*
Has a biting tongue.”!!!!!!!!!!!!!!!!!!

“**A***n angry man is always,*
Fearful.”!!!!!!!!!!!!!!!!!!!!!!!!!!!!!!!!!!!!!

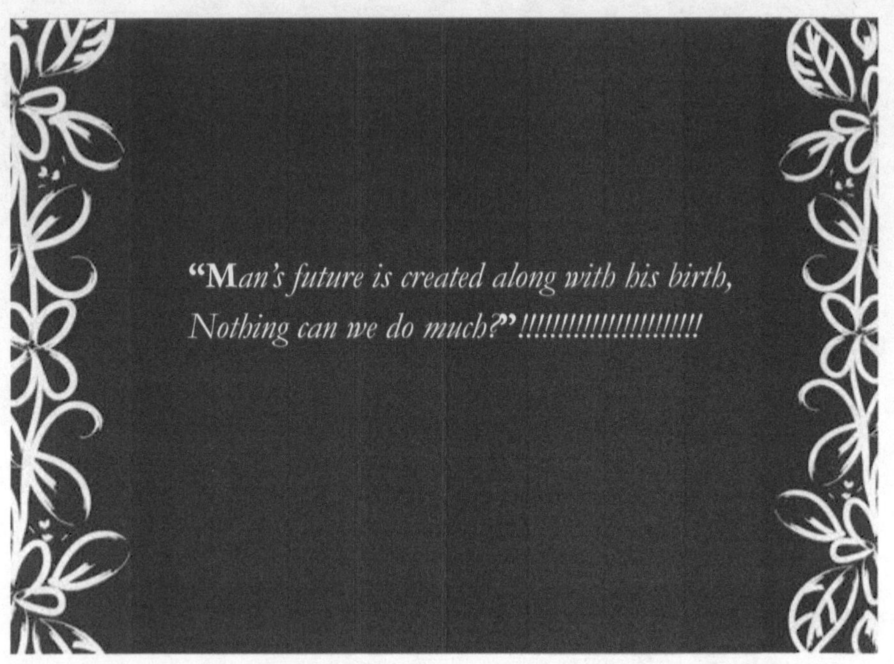

"When you're mature, you buy peace,
You embrace generocity
And shower forgiveness." !!!!!!!!!!!!!!!!!!!!!

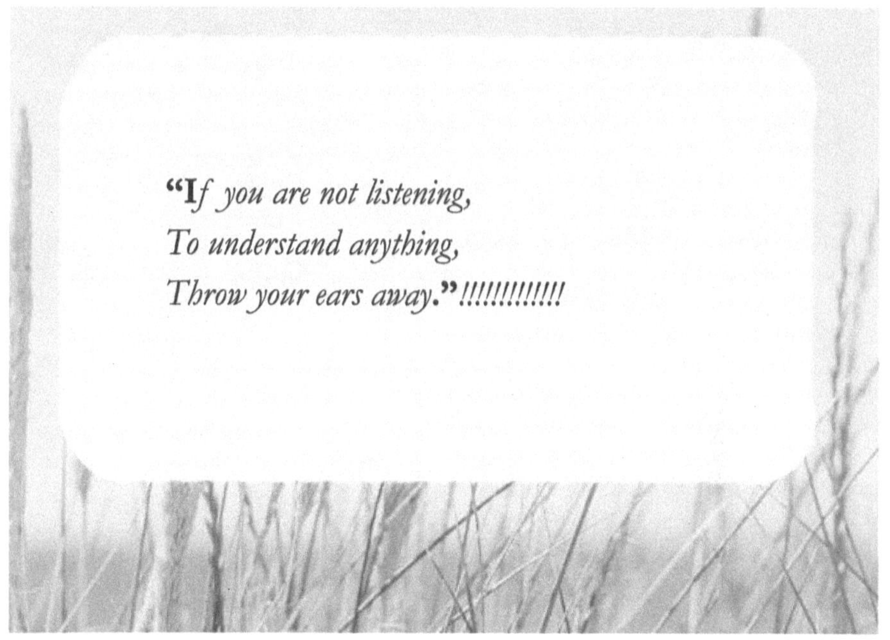

*“**I**f you are not listening,*
To understand anything,
Throw your ears away.” *!!!!!!!!!!!!!*

*“**T**ailor yourself*
But for yourself only.” *!!!!!!!!!!!!!!!!!!!!!!!!!!!*

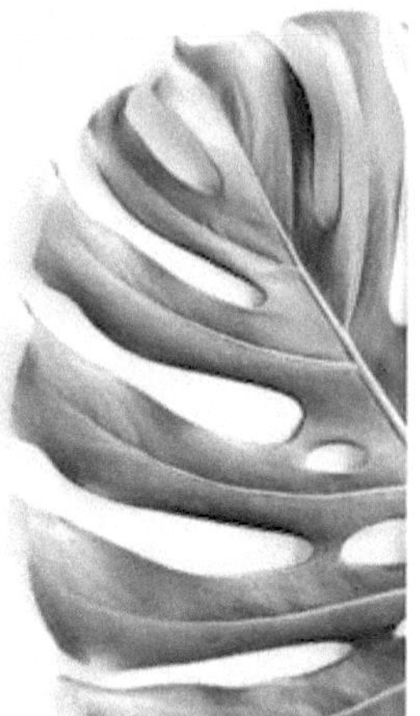

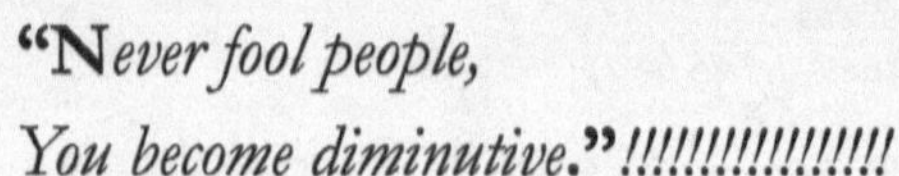

"*Never fool people,*
You become diminutive." !!!!!!!!!!!!!!!!!

*"**Y**ou are!!!!!!!!!*
Your beginnings
And endings too."!!!!!!!!!!!!!!!!!!!!

*"**A**lways avoid people who never apologise, in principle,,,,,,,,,,,,,,,*
For they live in a world with unjust Mindsets."!!!!!!!!!!!!!!

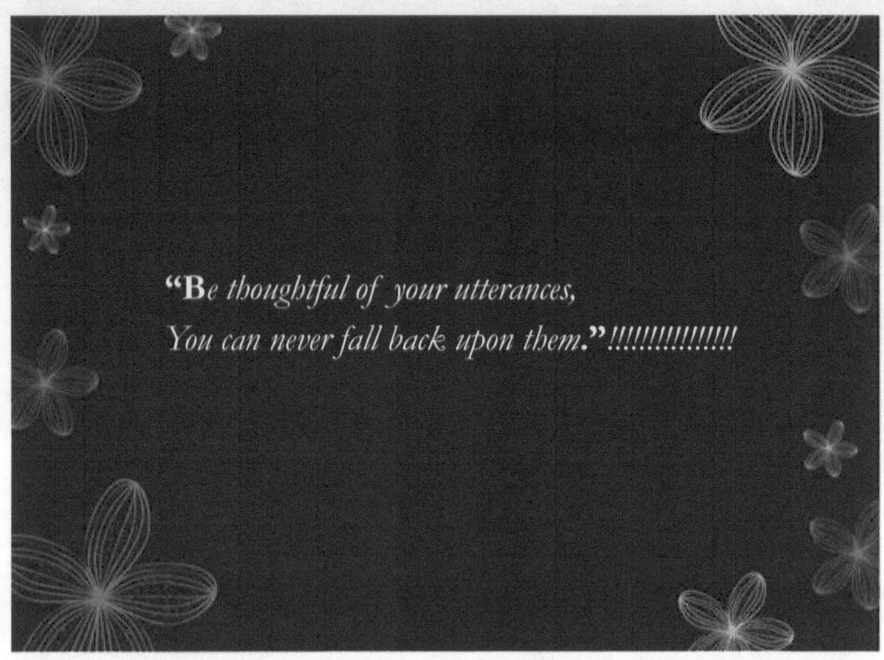

"**M***an is not finished, when he is defeated!!!!!!!!!!!!!!!!!*
He is finished, when he cannot face himself,
As also when he fails to face the World."!!!!!!!!!!!!!!!!!!!!!!!!

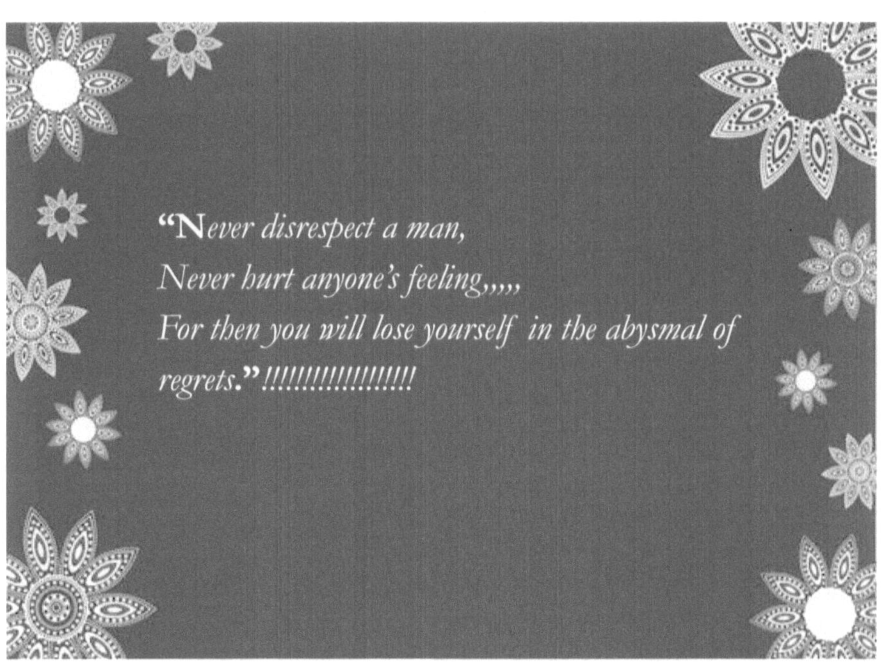
"Never disrespect a man,
Never hurt anyone's feeling,,,,,
For then you will lose yourself in the abysmal of regrets."!!!!!!!!!!!!!!!!!!

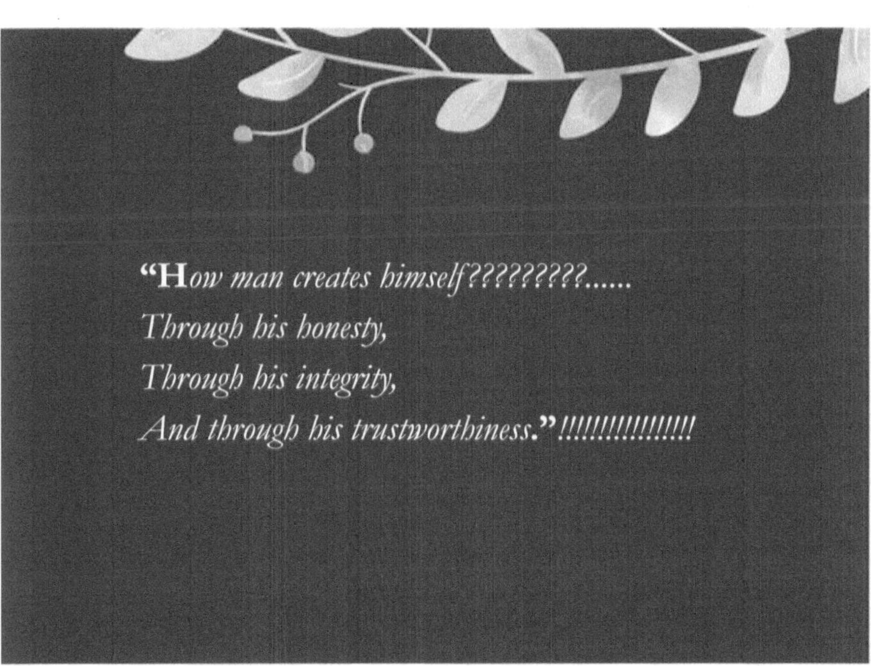
"How man creates himself??????????......
Through his honesty,
Through his integrity,
And through his trustworthiness."!!!!!!!!!!!!!!!!

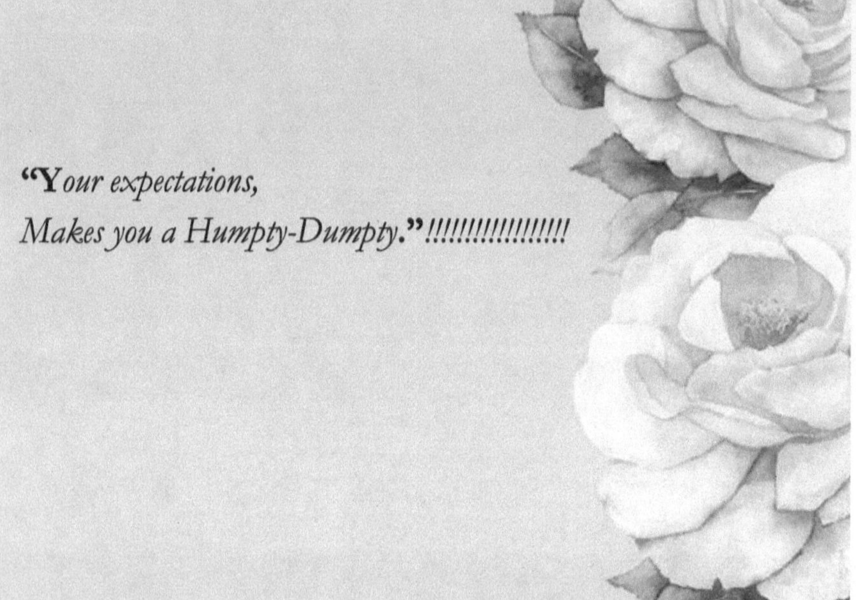
"Your expectations,
Makes you a Humpty-Dumpty."!!!!!!!!!!!!!!!!!

"To create something beautiful,
You have to loosen yourself, forget yourself
too."!!!!!!!!!!

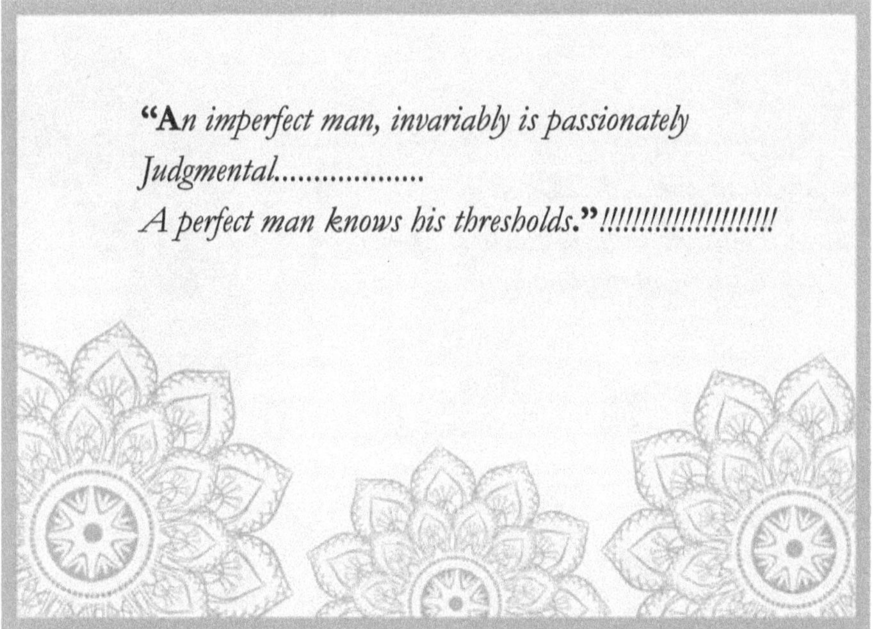
"An imperfect man, invariably is passionately
Judgmental..................
A perfect man knows his thresholds." !!!!!!!!!!!!!!!!!!!!!!

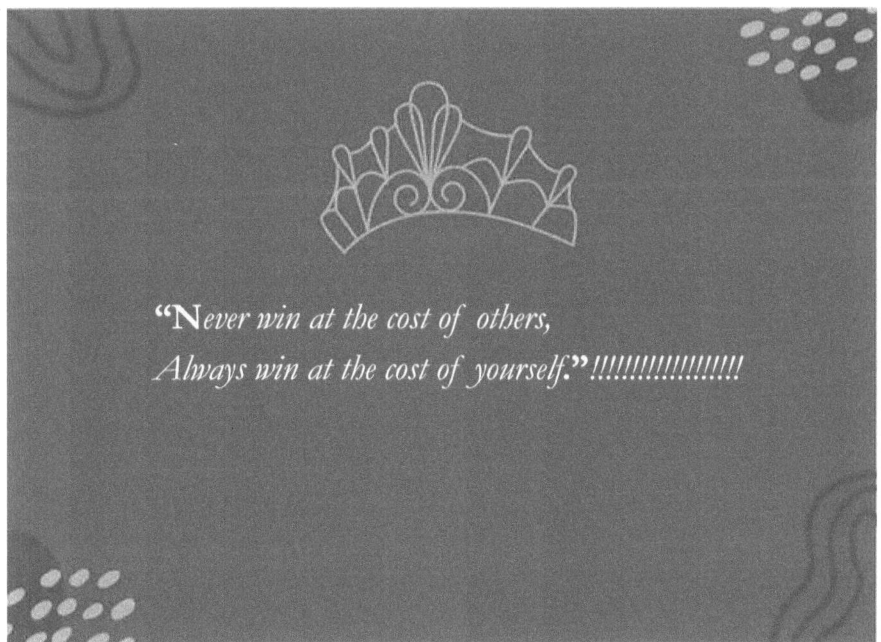
"Never win at the cost of others,
Always win at the cost of yourself." !!!!!!!!!!!!!!!!!!!

***"It is not the prerogative of man to punish or forgive anyone!!!!!!!!!!!!!!!!!!!!!!!
He is only given the mandate to live a clean and simple life."!!!!!!!!!!!!!!!!!!!!!!!!!!!!!***

***"Neither can you learn laziness,
Nor can you unlearn it,,,,,,,,,,,,,,,,,,,,,,,,,
Mans nerve endings rule the roost."!!!!!!!!!!!!!!***

“**B***eware with people who are noisy,*
For they always prove hallow and
shallow.” *!!!!!!!!!!!!*

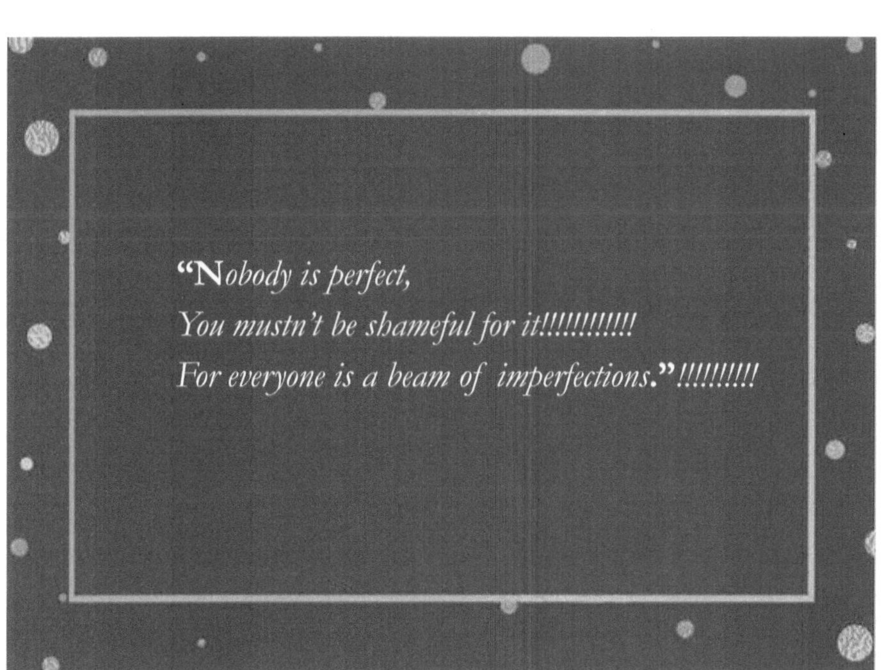

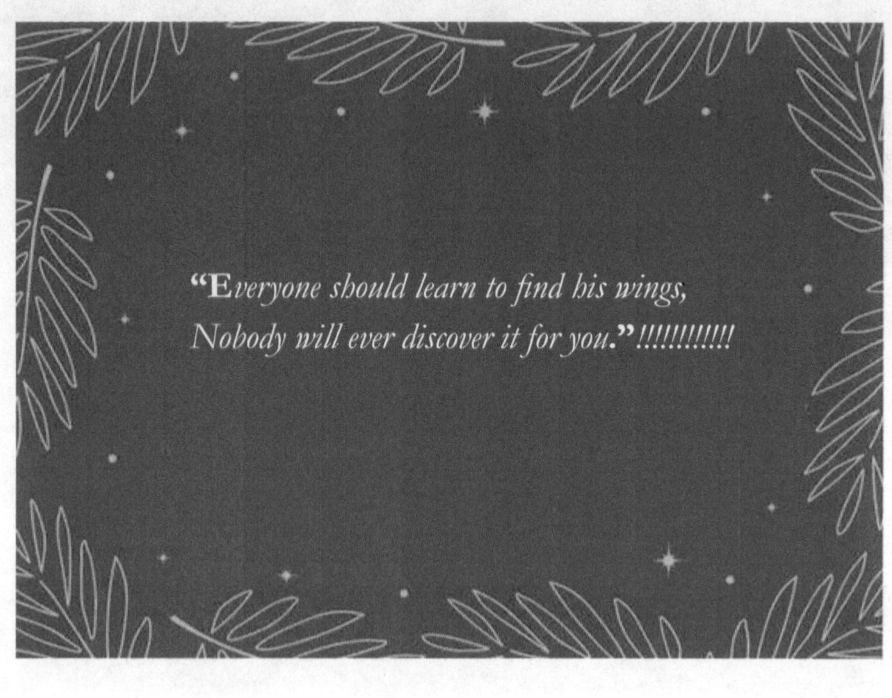

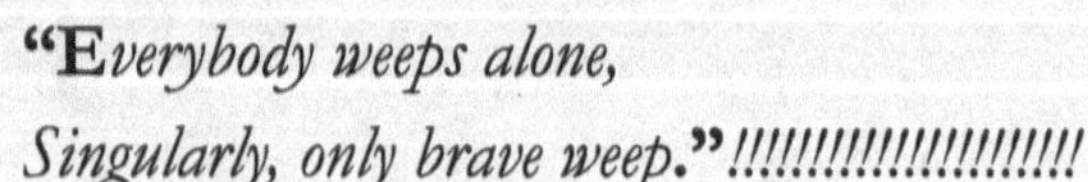
“E*verybody weeps alone,*
Singularly, only brave weep.” !!!!!!!!!!!!!!!!!!!!!!!!

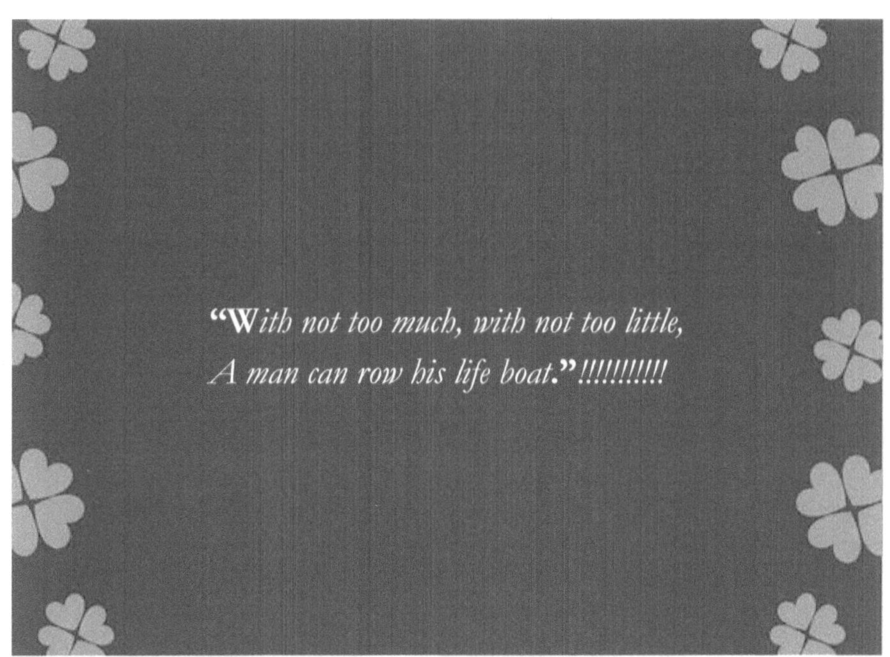
"With not too much, with not too little,
A man can row his life boat."!!!!!!!!!!!

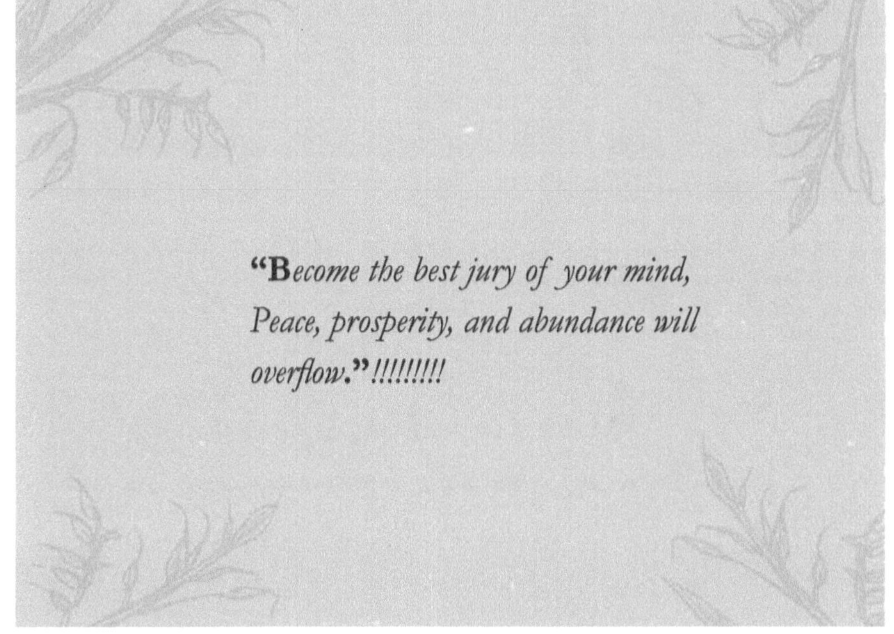
"Become the best jury of your mind,
Peace, prosperity, and abundance will
overflow."!!!!!!!!!

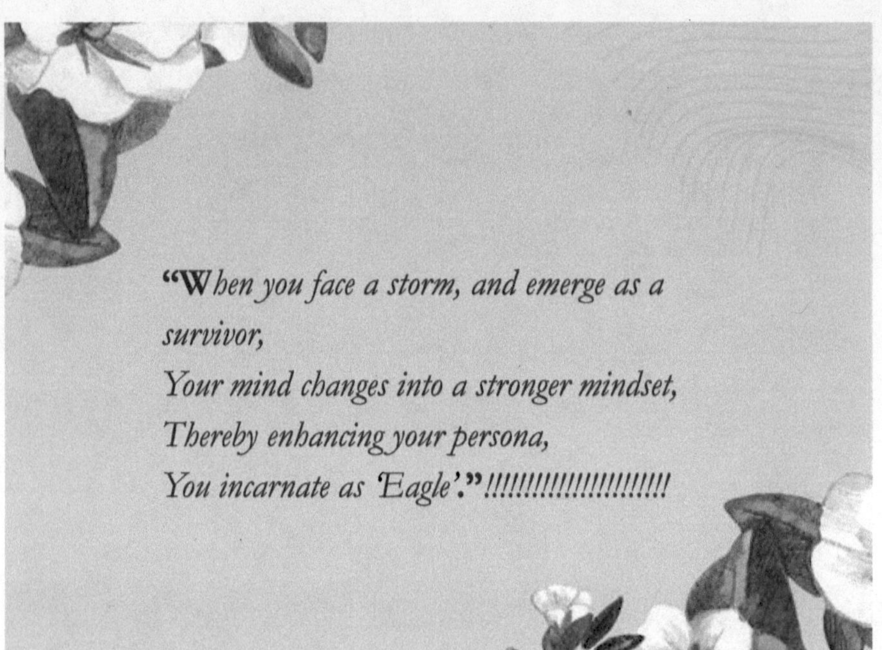

*"**W**hen you face a storm, and emerge as a survivor,*
Your mind changes into a stronger mindset,
Thereby enhancing your persona,
You incarnate as 'Eagle'." !!!!!!!!!!!!!!!!!!!!!!!

*"**M**uch of man's problems prove illusiory,*
Man's mind is a web of entanglements.......
He is created such." !!!!!!!!!!!!!!!!!!!!!!!!!!!!!!

*"**N**obody can bring your story to life,*
You necessarily ought to be your Artist." !!!!!!!!!!!!!!!!

*"**Y**our shouts portray,*
That you are a man with deep insecurities." !!!!!!!!!!!!

"Choices for man are
Made in Heavens."!!!!!!!!!!!!

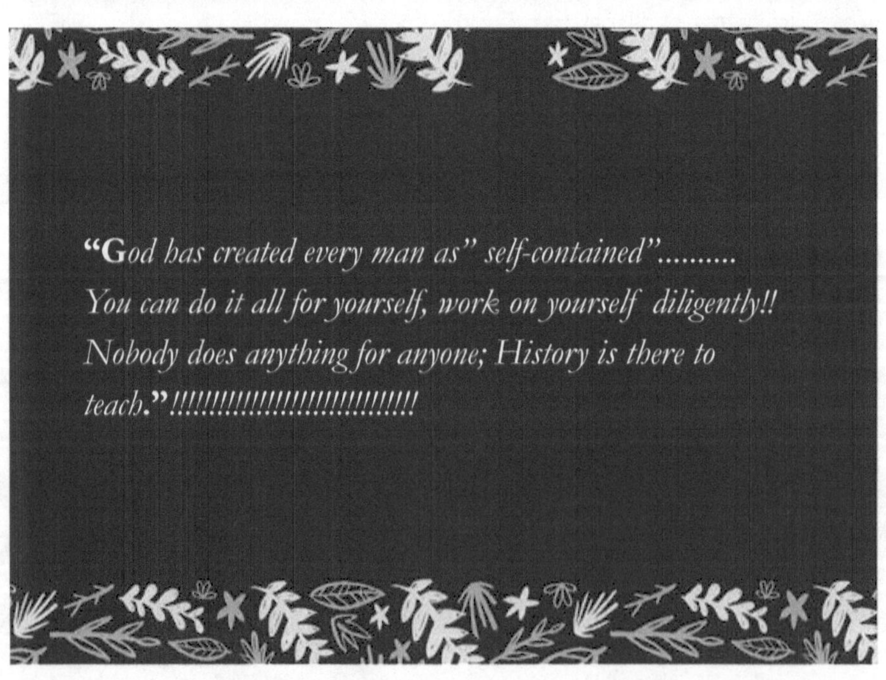
"God has created every man as" self-contained"..........
You can do it all for yourself, work on yourself diligently!!
Nobody does anything for anyone; History is there to
teach."!!!!!!!!!!!!!!!!!!!!!!!!!!!!!!!!

"***N**ever compete,*
We don't need it,
It denudes a spirited man."*!!!!!!!!!!*

"***S**tand up, and be counted.................*
Never be a weakling."*!!!!!!!!!!!!!!!!!!!!!!!!!!*

"**A***lways celebrate idleness,*
Without being guilty,
God never intended man as a machine." !!!!!!!!!!!!!!!!!!!!!!!!!!!!!!!

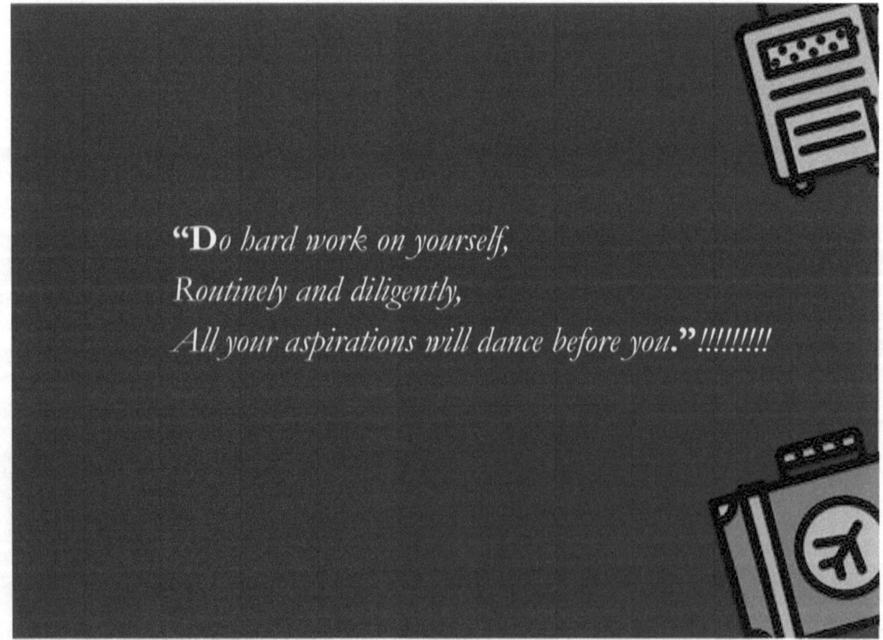

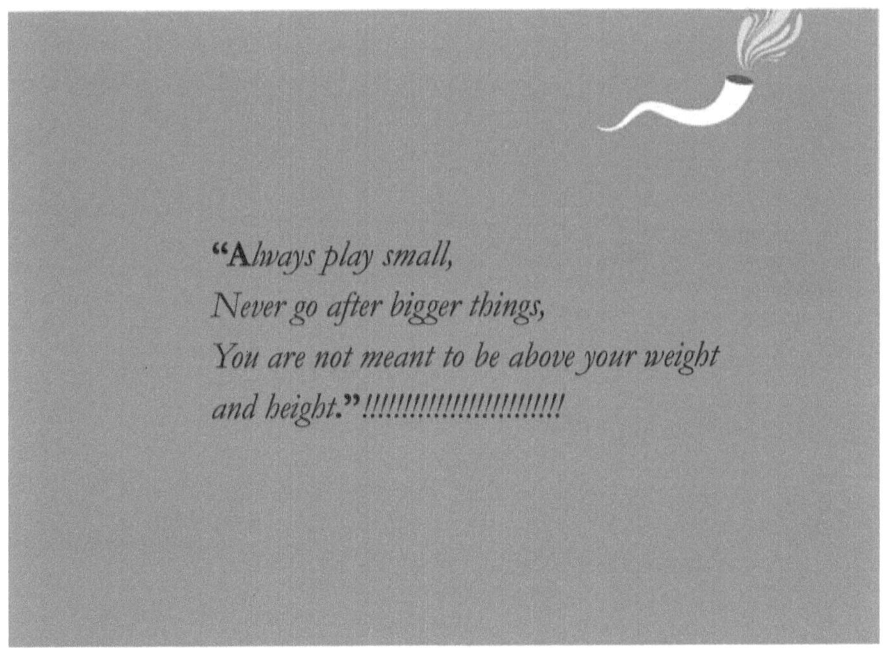

"**A***lways play small,*
Never go after bigger things,
You are not meant to be above your weight and height." *!!!!!!!!!!!!!!!!!!!!!!!!!*

"**F***or managing more in less time,*
You have to prioritise focus." *!!!!!!!!!!!!!!!!!!!!!!!!*

"O*ne should always pity*
A stupid man,
*For he is helpless with his mind.***"**!!!!!!!!!!!!!!!!!!

"T*hough stupidity harms,*
It is an innocence............
*Never punish a stupid.***"**!!!!!!!!!!!!!!!!!

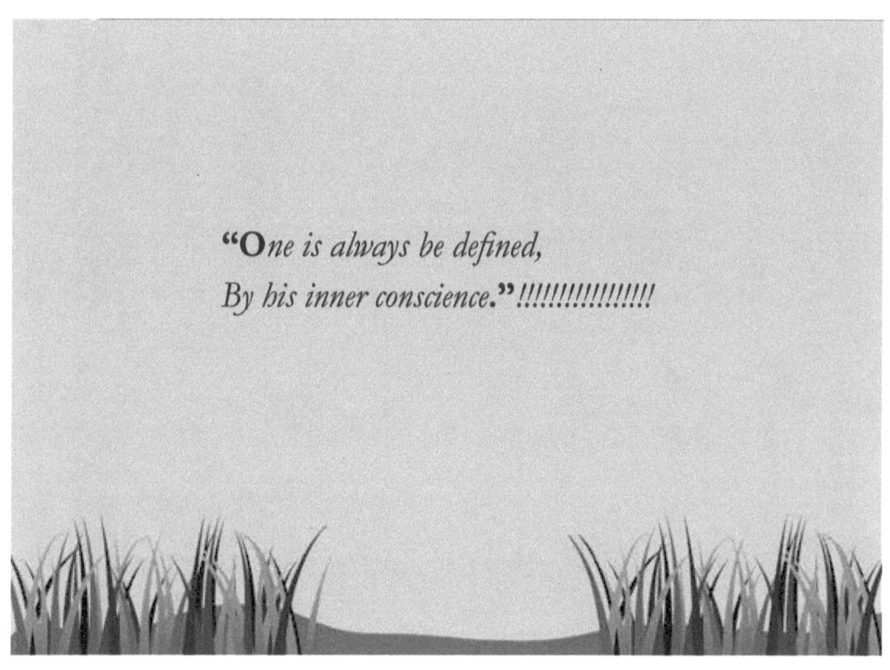

"**O***ne is always be defined,*
By his inner conscience." !!!!!!!!!!!!!!!!!

"**N***ever trust a man who is greedy.*" !!!!!!!!!!!!!!!!!

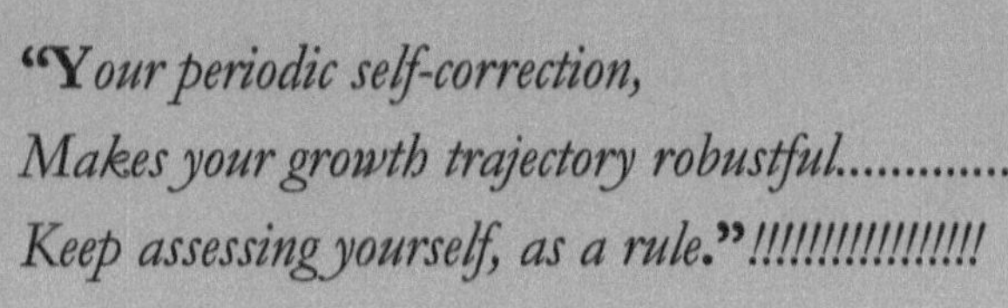

"Y*our periodic self-correction,*
Makes your growth trajectory robustful.............
Keep assessing yourself, as a rule."!!!!!!!!!!!!!!!!!

"A *man never helps anyone,*
Even when forthcoming, it comes in a selfish garb."!!!!!!!!!

"N*ever be a liar, For yourself.*"!!!!!!!!!!!!!!!!!!!!!!!!!

"A*lways be ready to reap the dividends of your mistakes.*"!!!!!!!!!!!!!!!!!!!!!!!!!!!!!

"**B***e selfish, it is good...........*
But not by harming others,,,,,,,,,,,,,,,,,,
Your selfishness must die unto
yourself." !!!!!!!!!!!!!!!!!!!!

"**W***hat constitutes your winning spree???????*
Your courage..........
Tenacity...............
Passion.............
Risking capacity...........
And, also so!!!!!!!!!!!Commitment." !!!!!!!!!!!!!!!!!!

"Never scold
An ignorant man
For you reap misfortunes."!!!!!!!!!!!!!!!!!!!!!

"Surround yourself with people
Who talk less And understand more,
Your peace will reverberate."!!!!!!!!!!!!!!!!!!

"**A** *Man is born at a chosen hour,*
And since, everything happens in an hour that is
'Chosen'." *!!!!!!!!!!!!!!!!!!*

"**T***oo many Rejections,*
Extends a man towards Acceptance." *!!!!!!!!!!!!!!!!!!*

"**N***ever overcommit yourself,*
You reap depression and guilt."*!!!!!!!!!!!!!!!!!!!*

"**A** *man who is on a look out to please everybody,*
Has a small soul!!!!!!!!!!!!!!!!!
He lacks a mindset."*!!!!!!!!!!!!!!!!!!!!!!!!!!!!!!!!!!!*

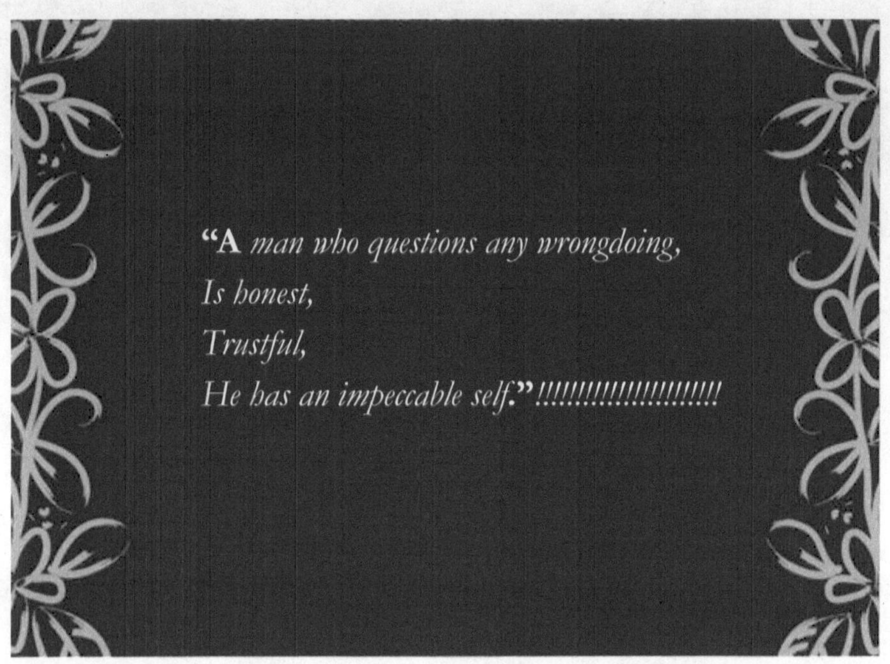
"A man who questions any wrongdoing,
Is honest,
Trustful,
He has an impeccable self."!!!!!!!!!!!!!!!!!!!!!!!

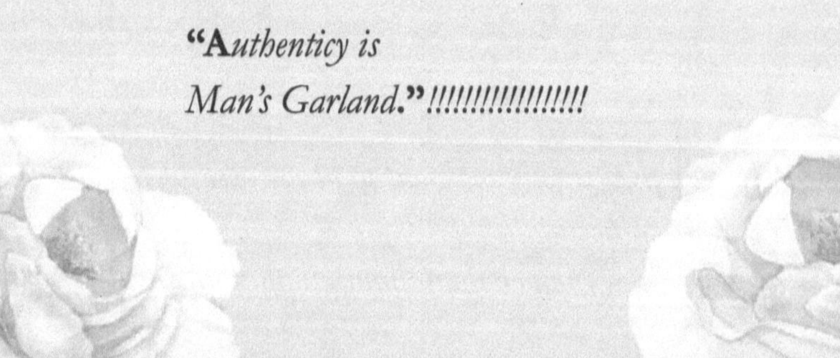
"Authenticy is
Man's Garland."!!!!!!!!!!!!!!!!!!

"**M***an is not made for an unlimited version of his pursuits!!!!!!!!
An intelligent man is one who knows his thresholds.*"!!!!!!!!!!!!

"**G***od is Lucky for Man.*"!!!!!!!!!!!!!!!!!

"**I***f you believe in yourself...........*
You just need no other conviction."*!!!!!!!!!!!!!!!!!!!!*

"**T***oo much imagination,*
Broods inaction,,,,,,,,,,,
A high value risk."*!!!!!!!!!!!!!!!!!!!!*

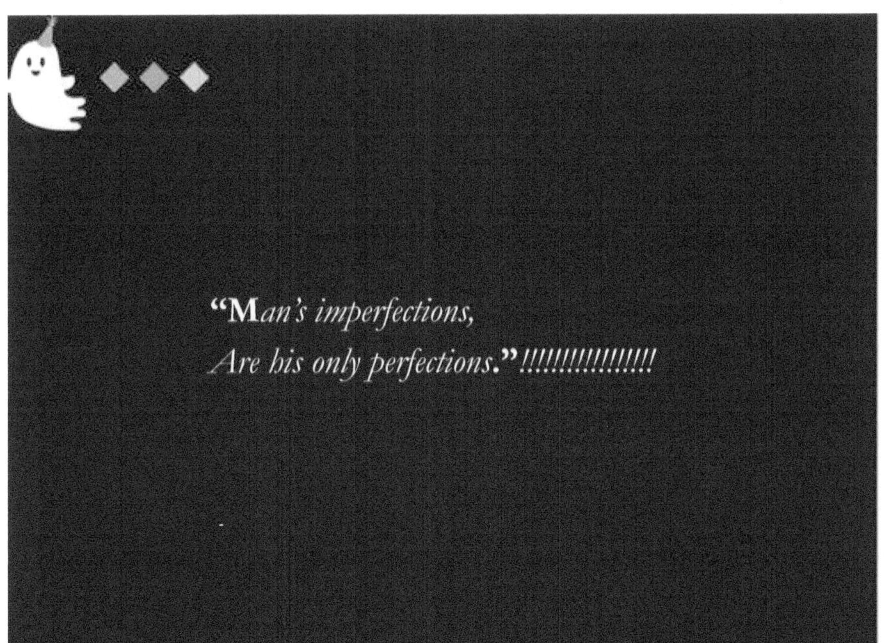
"Man's imperfections,
Are his only perfections."!!!!!!!!!!!!!!!!

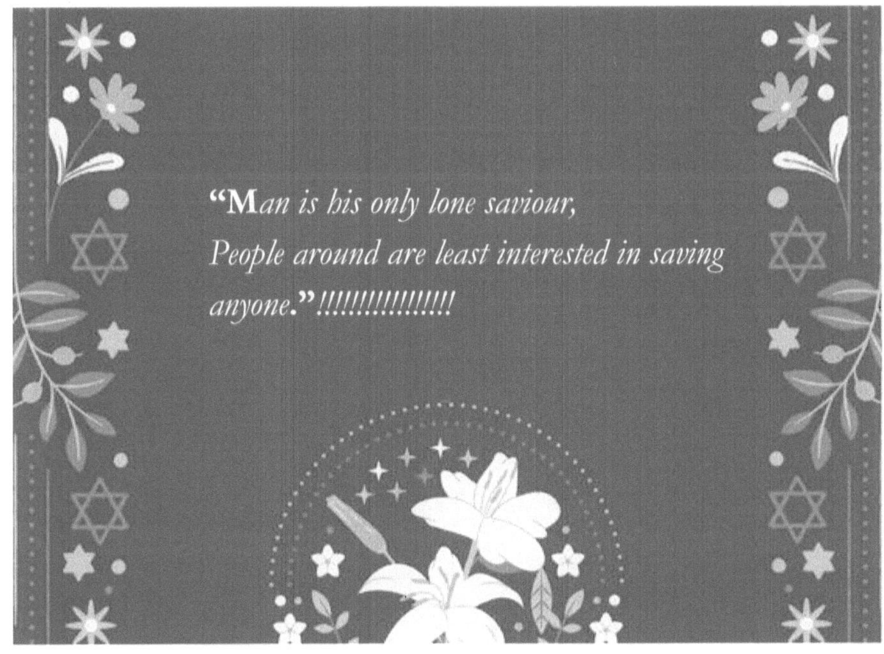
"Man is his only lone saviour,
People around are least interested in saving
anyone."!!!!!!!!!!!!!!!!

"A man should be always
Be serving in his attributes,
The more you uplift,
The more are you kicked off,
Upwards!!!!!!!!!!!!!!!!
Solemnly?"!!!!!!!!!!!!!!!!!!!!!

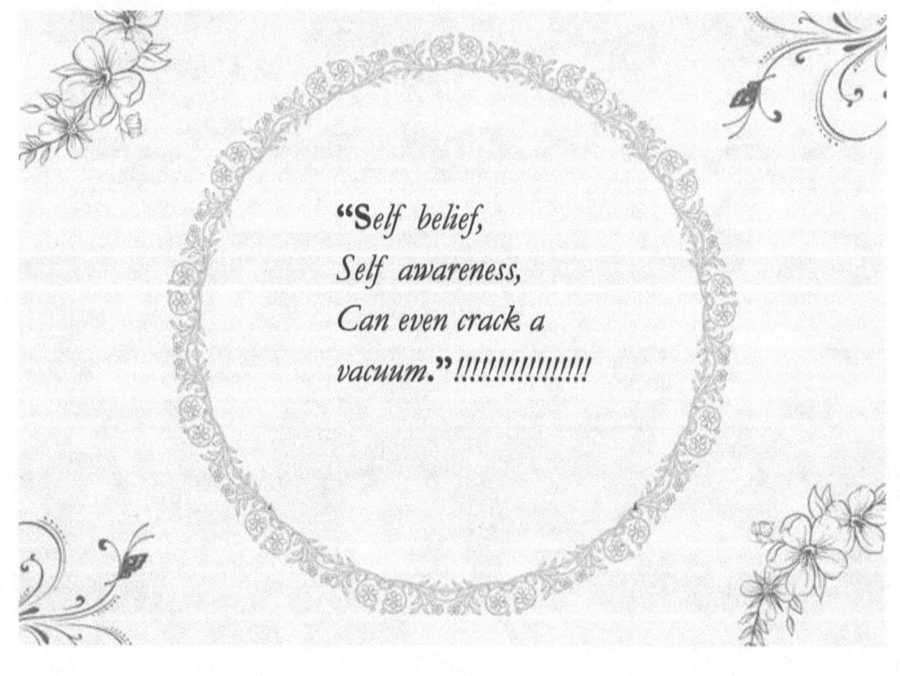
"Self belief,
Self awareness,
Can even crack a
vacuum."!!!!!!!!!!!!!!!!!

*"**W**isely use these trio to propel yourself....*
Your discipline,
Your patience,
And your time." !!!!!!!!!!!!!!!!!!!!!!!!!!!!!

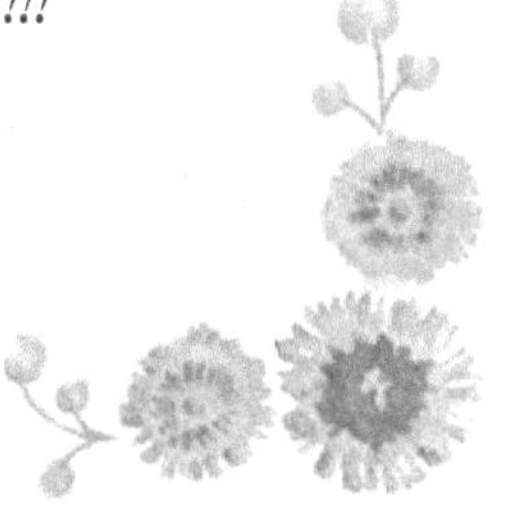

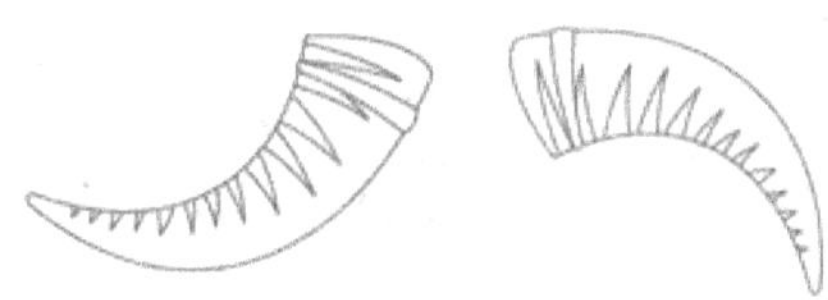

"**A** *Give is more Humil,*
Than a take,
Always be in a search for uplifting others." !!!!!!!!!!!!!!

“Everything of a man is blessed,
Except his bad temper.” !!!!!!!!!!!!!!!!!

“Love your struggles,
Be engaged with it passionately.” !!!!!!!!!!!!!!!!!

*"**Y**our thoughts become your reality,*
Provided you have manifested deep
resilience." !!!!!!!!!!!!!!!!!!!!!!!!!!!!!!!

*"**I**f a man keeps moving forward............*
Howsoever slow,
He is living life wisely...........
He will end up with everything." !!!!!!!!!!!!!!!!!!!

"T*he greatest strength which a man should portray???*
He ought to be humil,
And be fast enough to admit his weaknesses!!!!!!!!!!!!
*A transparent attitude always pays in life.***"** *!!!!!!!!!!!!!!!!*

"A *man shouldn't always play to win,*
He should promisingly incorporate a losers mindset too!!!!!!!!!!
In your victory you become blind...........
*In your defeat you become sublime.***"** *!!!!!!!!!!!!!!!!!*

*"**M**an is incarnated to face challenges,*
If God was not promised a cakewalk,!!!!!!
Why men?" !!

*"**M**an is primarily a shaky personality..........*
He has varying degrees of shifting doubts." !!!!!!!!

*"**H**e who can write off his past,*
Is a spineless entity." !!!!!!!!!!!!!!!!!!!!

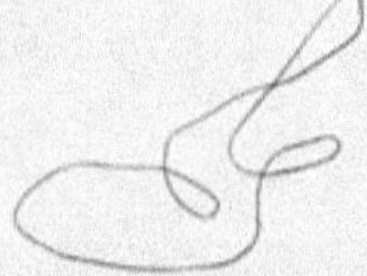

*"**Y**our Self must be,*
Your dearest Pinnacle." !!!!!!!!!!!!!!!!!!

"**P***eople are in a habit for crying for the person,*
Who hurts them most!!!!!!!!!!!!!!
This is a dialect of human nature." *!!!!!!!!!!!!!!!!!!*

"**A** *man who is in command of his responses,*
Becomes a wise man." *!!!!!!!!!!!!!!!!!!!!!!!!!!*

"H*onoring promises,*
Makes a man trustworthy." !!!!!!!!!!!!!!!!!!!!

"T*hrough the telescopes we bring our*
Future admist ourselves,
Should we not self-pity man for this jingoism?" !!!!!!!!!!!!!!!

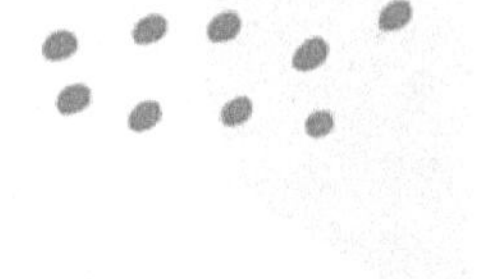

“Every man is thrown flattened once, twice or thrice By life,
Your arising is what matters.” !!!!!!!!!!!!!!!!!!!!!!!!!!

“Your instinct to put questions across
Is the single most pertinent answer of your vibes of self-betterment.” !!!!!!!!!!!!!!!!!!!!!!!!!!!!!!!!!!!!!!!

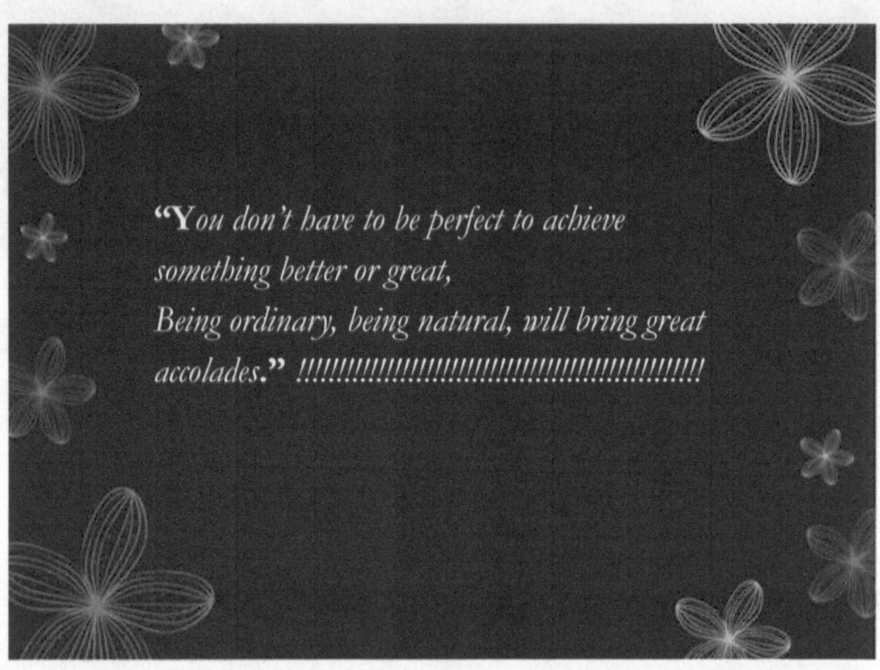
"You don't have to be perfect to achieve
something better or great,
Being ordinary, being natural, will bring great
accolades." !!

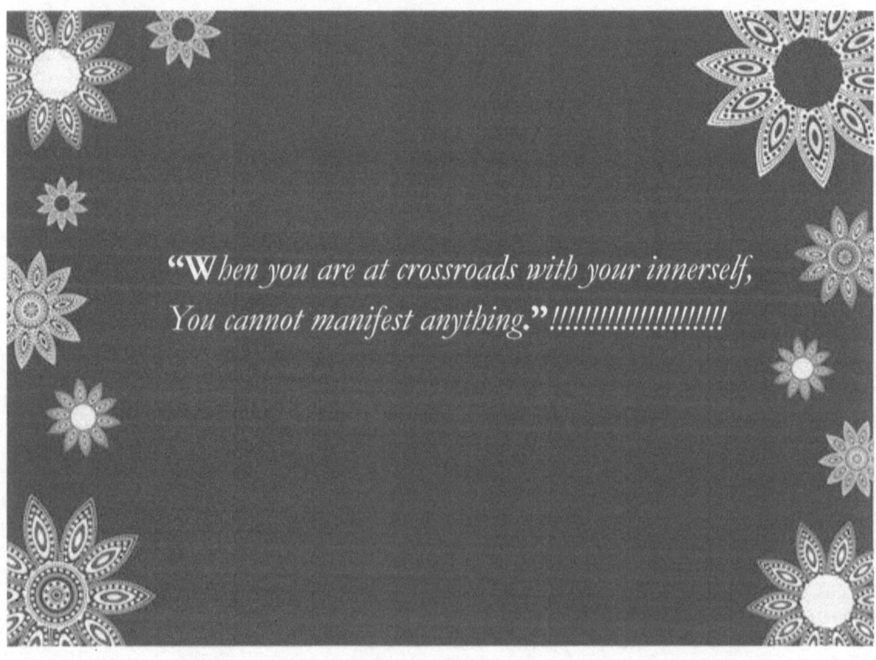
"When you are at crossroads with your innerself,
You cannot manifest anything."!!!!!!!!!!!!!!!!!!!!!!!

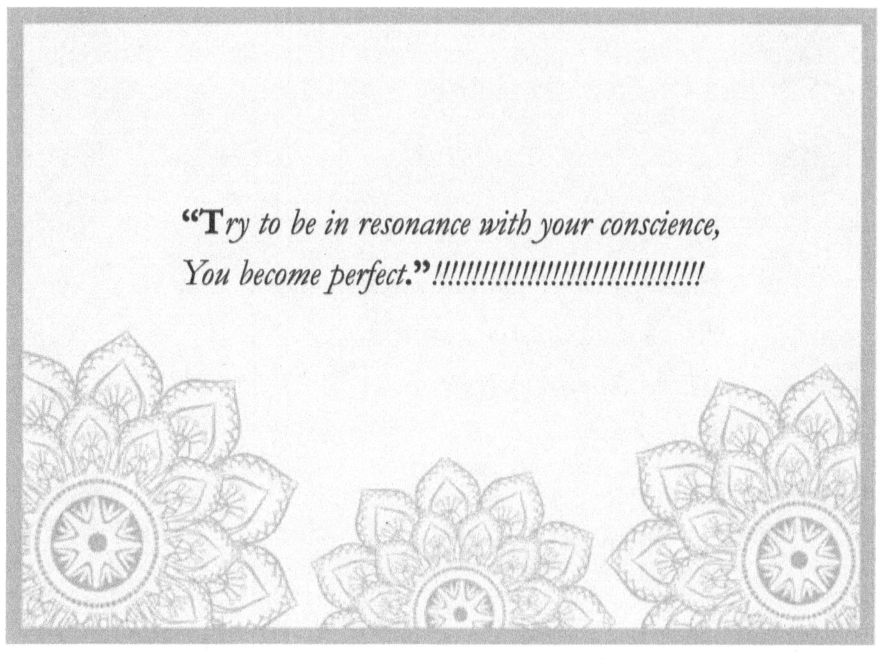

*"The problem with man is,
Most of the time he is ashamed of
himself."* !!!!!!!!!!!!!

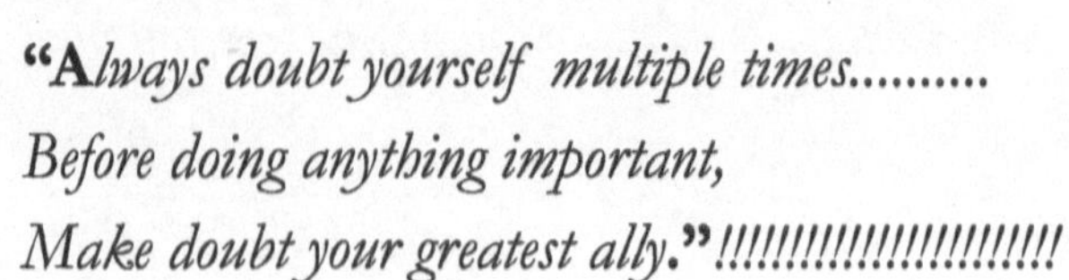

*"**A**lways doubt yourself multiple times..........*
Before doing anything important,
Make doubt your greatest ally." !!!!!!!!!!!!!!!!!!!!!!!!!

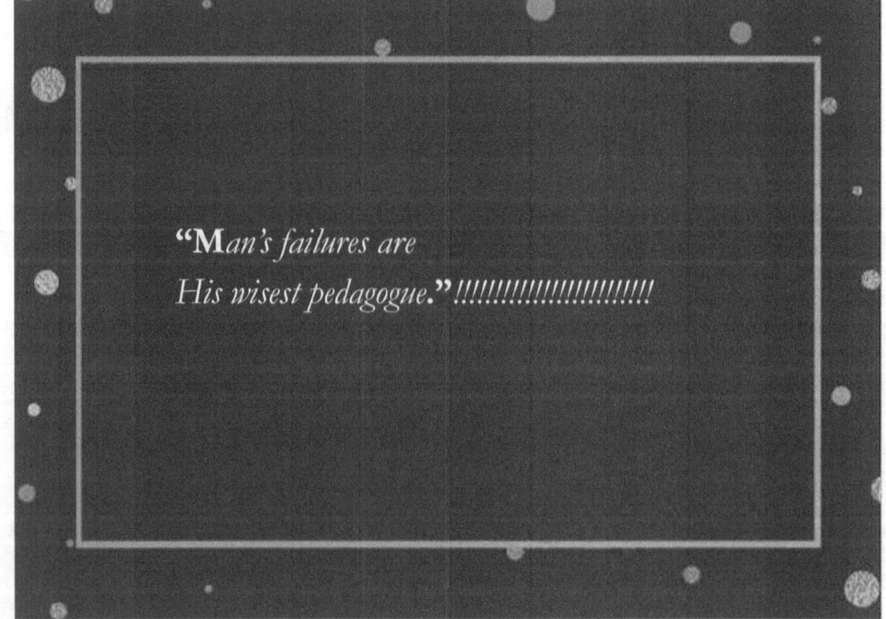

*"**M**an's failures are*
His wisest pedagogue." !!!!!!!!!!!!!!!!!!!!!!!!!

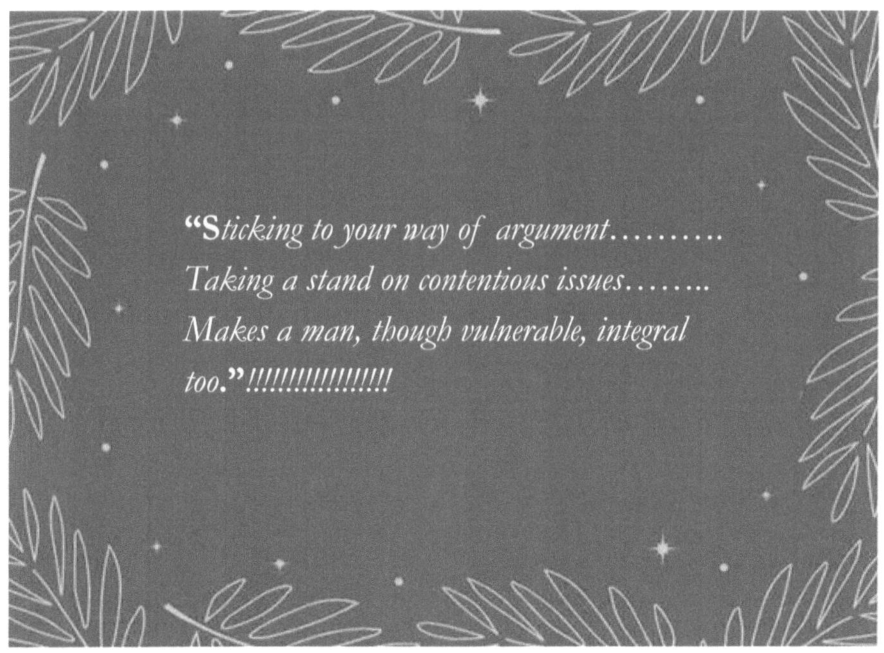

“**S***elf-belief is our greatest aura stimulus.*”*!!!!!!!!!!!!!*

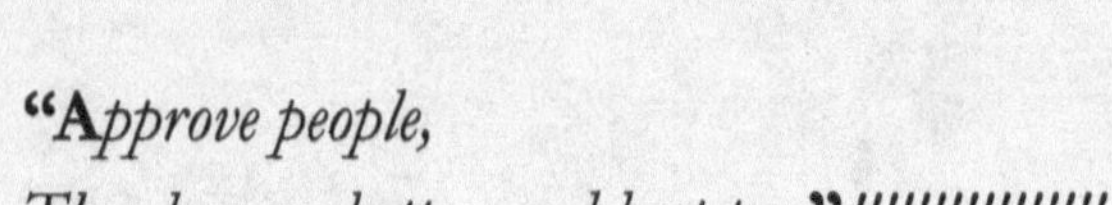

*“**A**pprove people,*
They become better, and best too.”!!!!!!!!!!!!!!!!

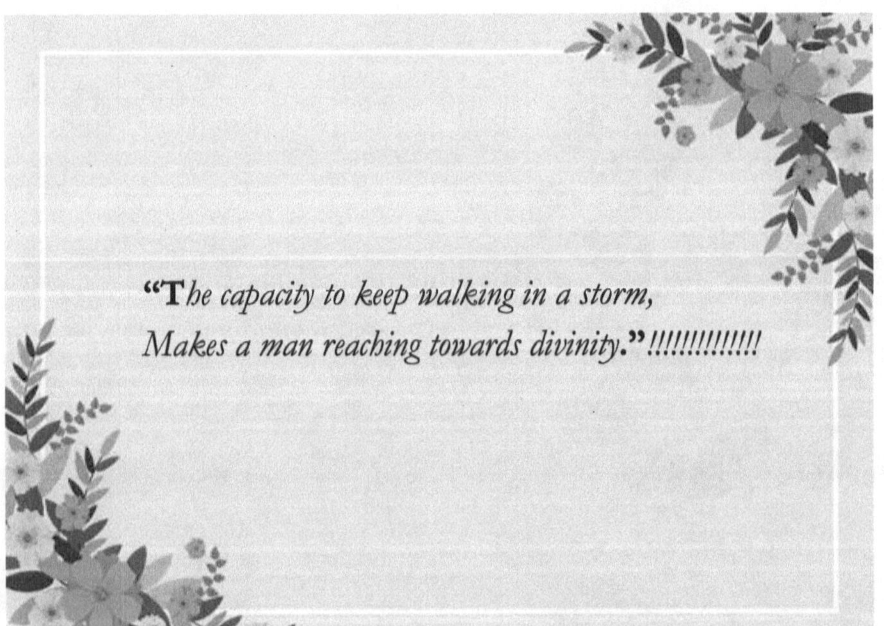

*“**T**he capacity to keep walking in a storm,*
Makes a man reaching towards divinity.”!!!!!!!!!!!!!!

"Man is basically a fearful creature...............
He can only overcome it by his willpower." !!!!!!!!!!!!!!!

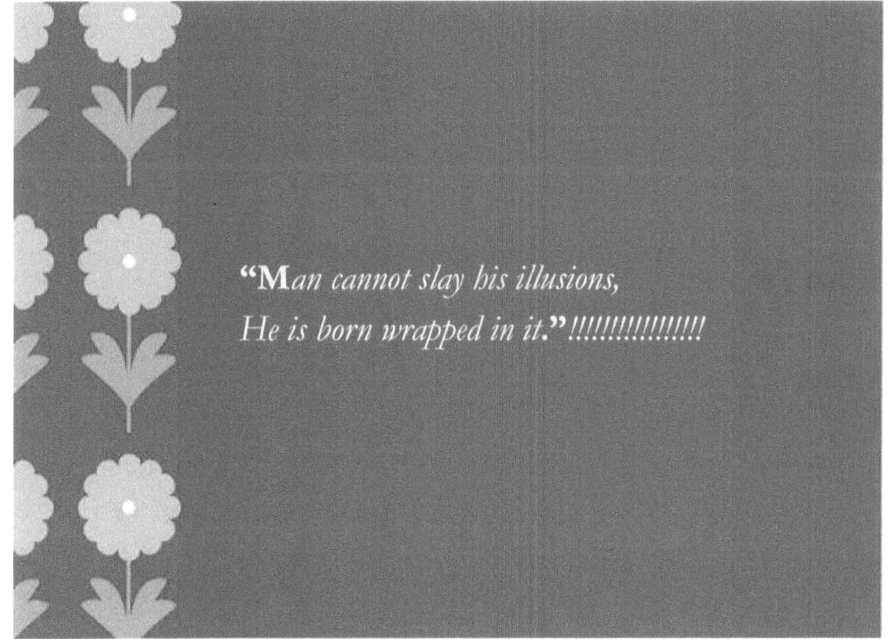
"Man cannot slay his illusions,
He is born wrapped in it." !!!!!!!!!!!!!!!!!

*"**M**an can only be awakened,
By the inner gushes of his
urges."* !!!!!!!!!!!!!

*"**Y**our grace is where,*
The courage resides." !!!!!!!!!!!!!!!!!

*"**Y**our confidence ought to be fearful,*
Of your overconfidence." !!!!!!!!!!!!!!!!!!!!!

"**M***an is primarily,*
A solitary reaper." *!!!!!!!!!!!!!!!!!!!*

"**M***an is killing himself,*
From the overdose of reason." *!!!!!!!!!!!!!!*

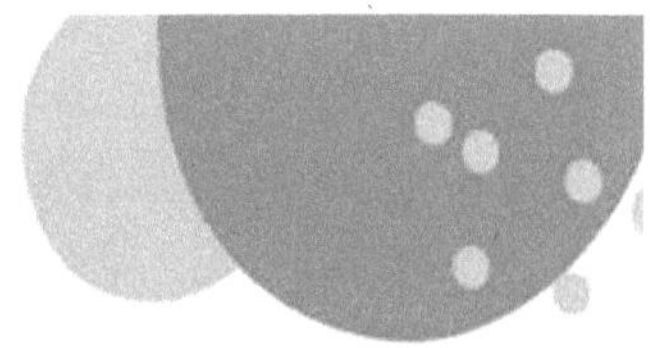

"Generosity always pulls you up,
It has a thrust." !!!!!!!!!!!!!!!!!!!!!!!!!!!!!

"Questioning Anything, or Anybody,
When need arise.........
Ought to be a rule." !!!!!!!!!!!!!!!!!!!

"**M***an earns self.....respect,*
Simply by trusting himself." !!!!!!!!!!!!!

"**A** *man standing alone always*
Appears taller." !!!!!!!!!!!!!!!!!!!!!!!!!!!!!!!!

"**A** *man who admits, he is fallible*
Is a thorough gentleman."*!!!!!!!!!!!!!!!!*

"**S***ufferance makes a*
Man brave."*!!!!!!!!!!!!!!!!!!!!!!*

"I*f you abide by your self-respect,*
*You will definitely respect others too.***"** *!!!!!!!!!!!!!!!*

"M*an's passion for life dictates his*
*success.***"** *!!!!!!!!!!!!!!!!*

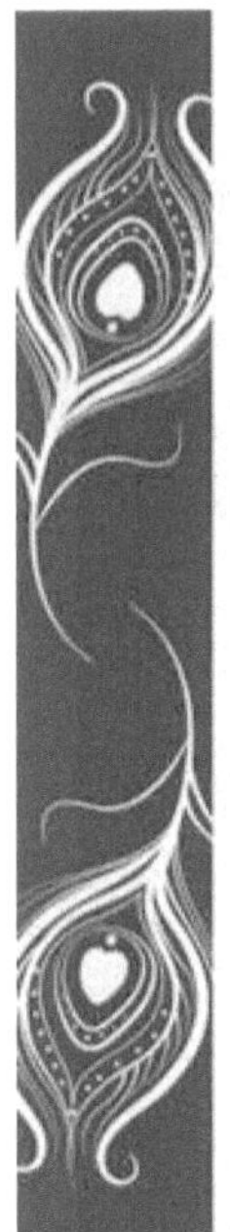

*"**H**ard work make a man sexually strong,*
Smart work makes a man sexually weaker."!!!!!!!!!!

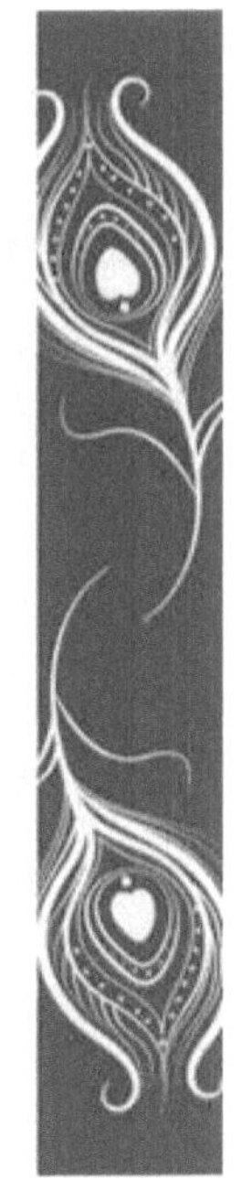

*"**T**he hardest voice for a man to overcome,*
Is his voice of guilt."!!!!!!!!!!!!!!

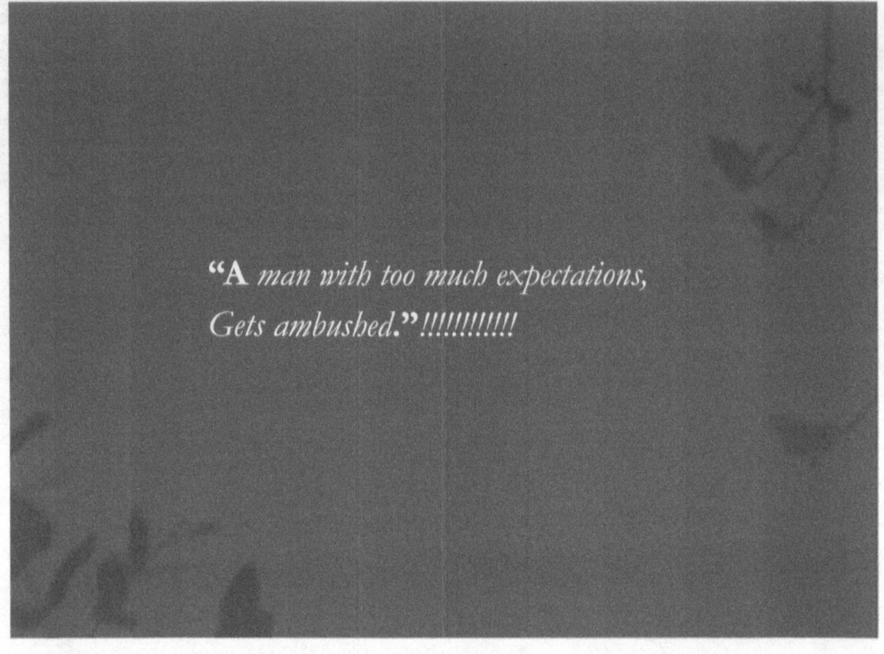
“**A** *man with too much expectations,*
Gets ambushed.” !!!!!!!!!!!!

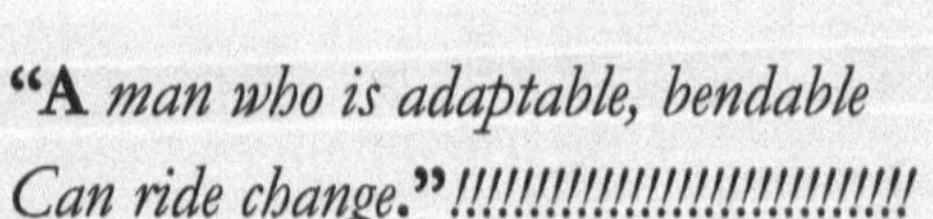
“**A** *man who is adaptable, bendable*
Can ride change.” !!!!!!!!!!!!!!!!!!!!!!!!!!!!!!!!

“**E***very strong man is a swimmer.........*
In water! In air! In vacuum too.” *!!!!!!!!!!!!!!!*

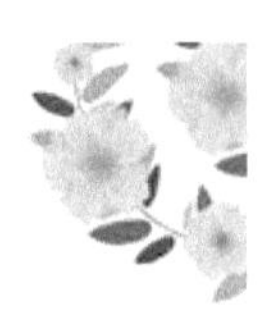

“**A** *great and fulfilled man,*
His least worried with his future.” *!!!!!!!!!!!*

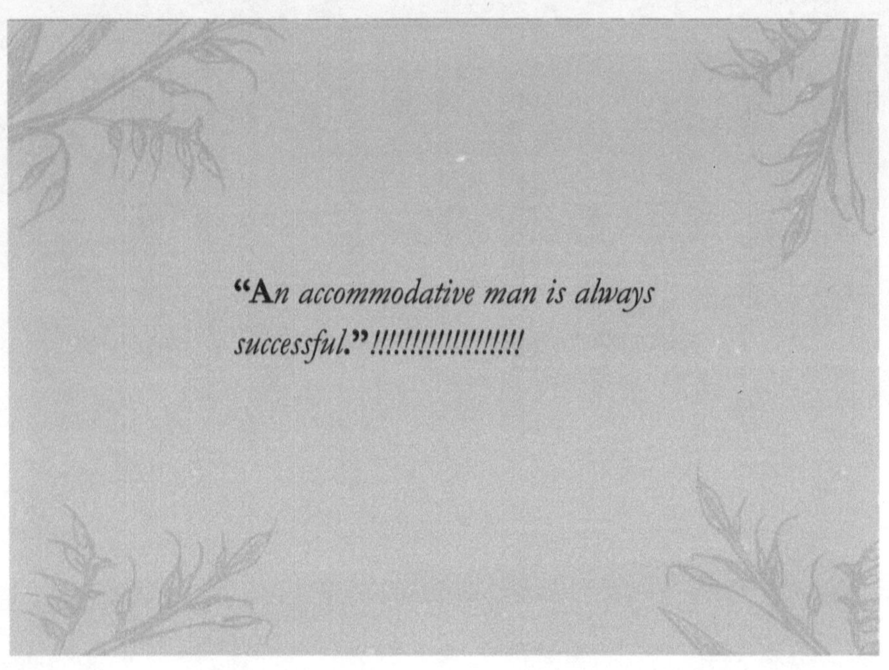

“**A***n accommodative man is always successful.*” *!!!!!!!!!!!!!!!!!!!*

“**W***hen a man learns to laugh at himself,*
He becomes a realist.” *!!!!!!!!!!!!!!!!!!!!!!!*

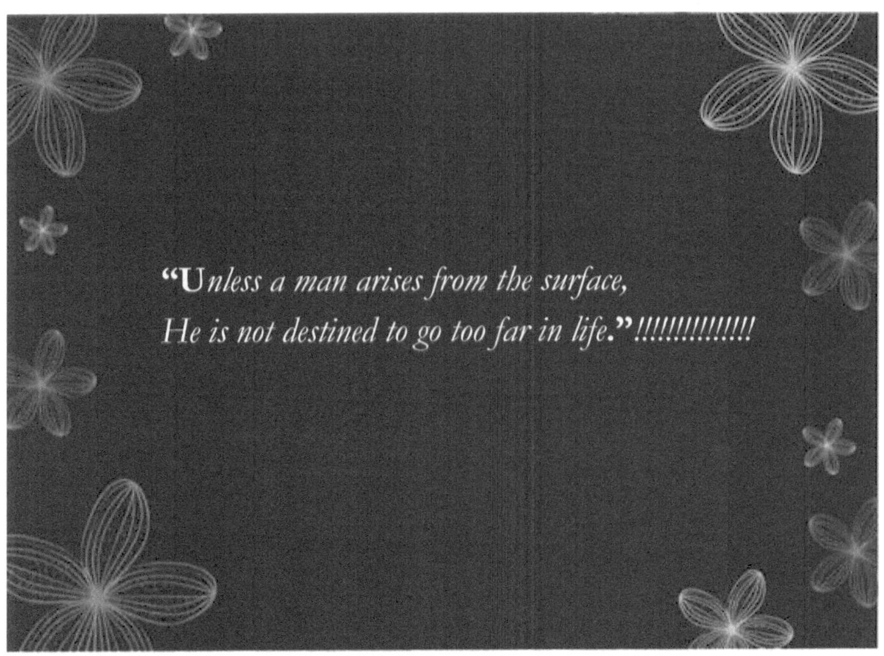
"Unless a man arises from the surface,
He is not destined to go too far in life."!!!!!!!!!!!!!!

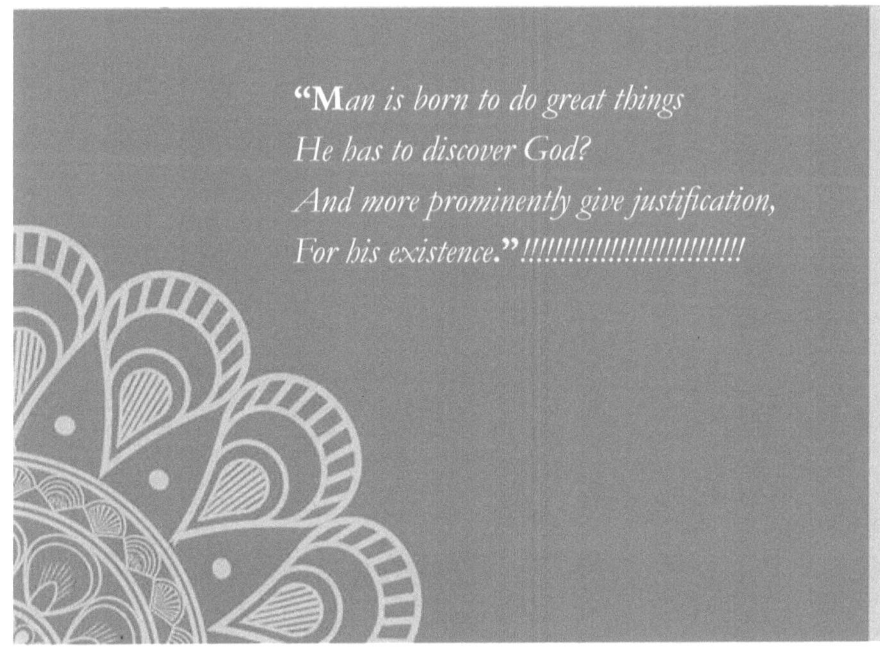
"Man is born to do great things
He has to discover God?
And more prominently give justification,
For his existence."!!!!!!!!!!!!!!!!!!!!!!!!!!!!

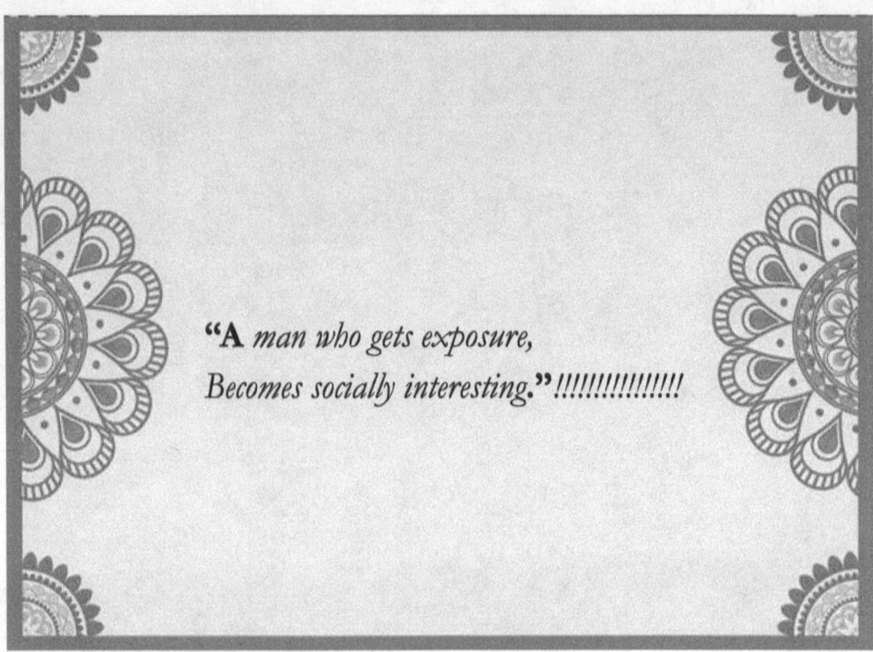
"**A** *man who gets exposure,*
Becomes socially interesting." !!!!!!!!!!!!!!!!

"**M***an is not born to prove anything,*
His placement is to live life integrally." !!!!!!!!!!!!

*"**W**iser be the man,*
Whose mind is open…ended."!!!!!!!!!!!!!!

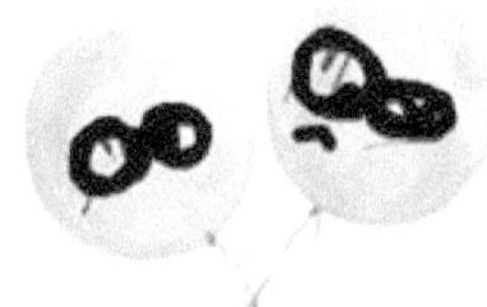

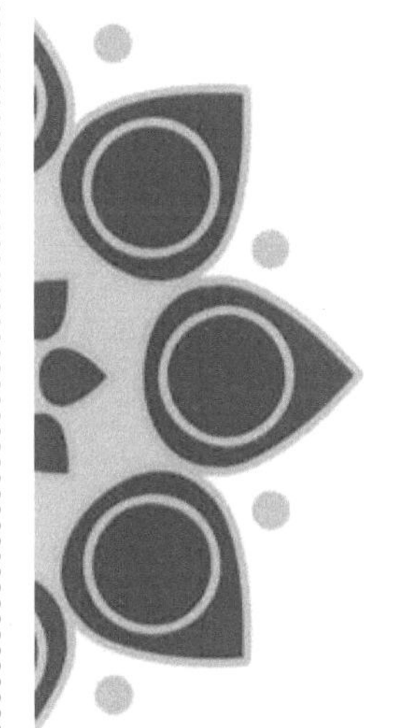

*"**I**n Forgiveness,*
Man's sanctity is hidden."!!!!!!!!!!!!!!!

*"**N**ever be in a hurry, to gulp your steps,*
Be a man used and tuned for taking small steps...............
At least, your destination becomes assured."!!!!!!!!!!!!!!!!!

*"**P**resent is man's embodiment."!!!!!!!*

"**A** *stressful man*
Is a hurried one too."!!!!!!!!

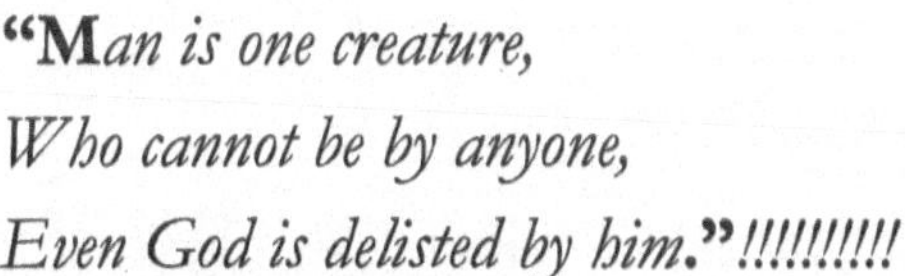

"**M***an is one creature,*
Who cannot be by anyone,
Even God is delisted by him."!!!!!!!!!!

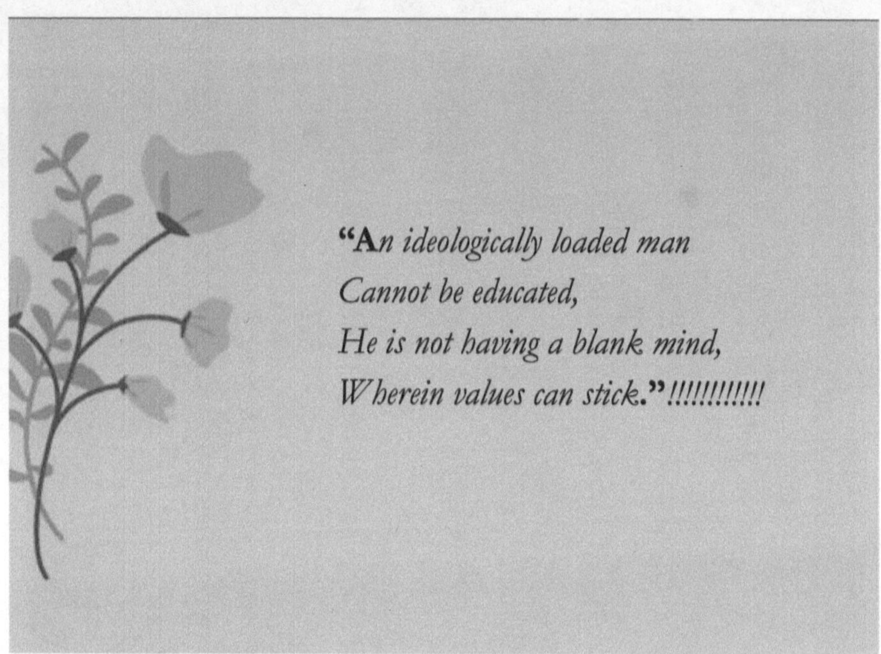
"An ideologically loaded man
Cannot be educated,
He is not having a blank mind,
Wherein values can stick."!!!!!!!!!!!

"With Ego.....
Man never Grows.......................
He become Diminutive."!!!!!!!!!!!!!!

"Ego bisects man's conscience."!!!!!!!!!!!!!!!!!

"You should pity on jealous people,
For they are killing themselves."!!!!!!!!!!!!!!!!!!!!!!!

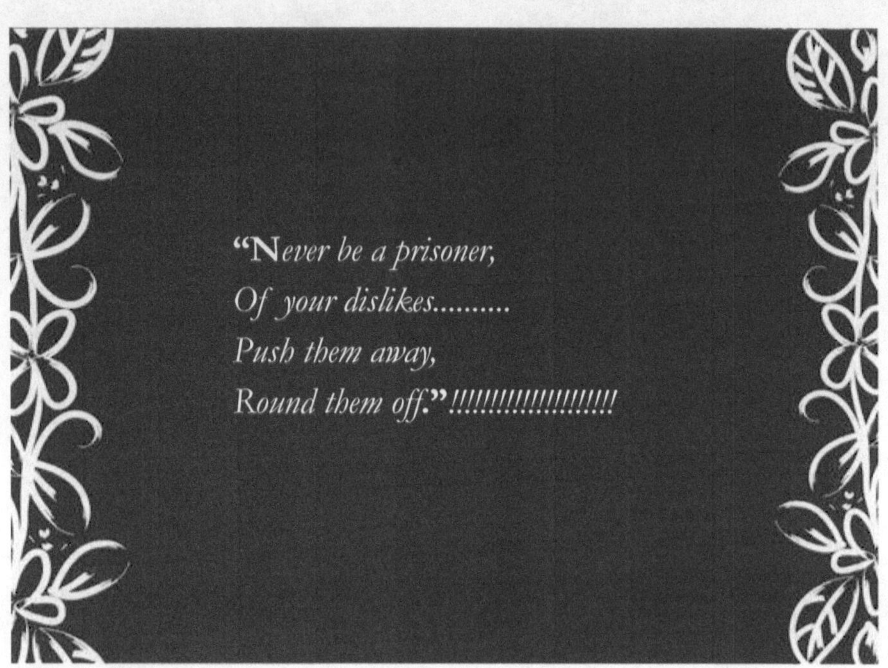
"Never be a prisoner,
Of your dislikes..........
Push them away,
Round them off."!!!!!!!!!!!!!!!!!!!!!

"Never laugh your last laugh...
Save it for adversity."!!!!!!!!!!!!!!!!!!

"**P***eople who are obsessed with public glare*
Are basically small souls." *!!!!!!!!!!!!!!!!!!!!!!!!!!!!*

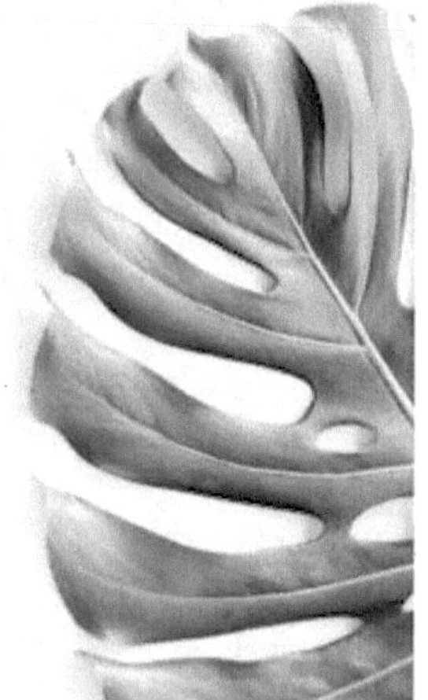

"**Y***our shoes are meant for you,*
Never try imagining it to gift it to
anyone." *!!!!!!!!!!*

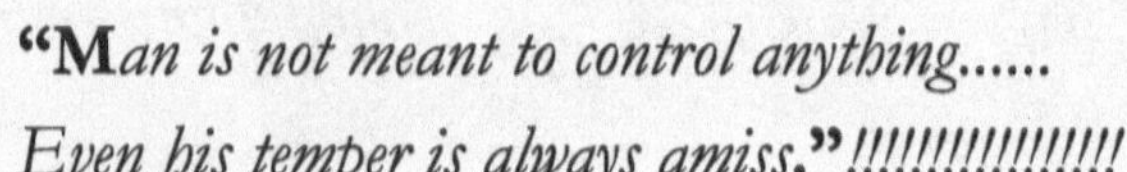

"**M***an is not meant to control anything......*
Even his temper is always amiss." *!!!!!!!!!!!!!!!!!*

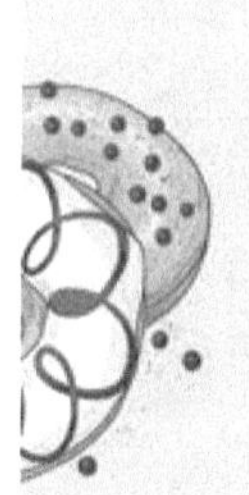

"I*f you become mature,*
You shed reactions
*A maturer man is never reactionary.***"** *!!!!!!!!!!!!!!!!!!*

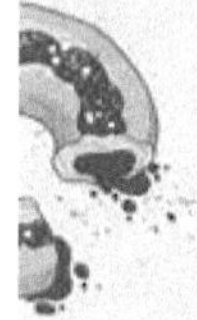

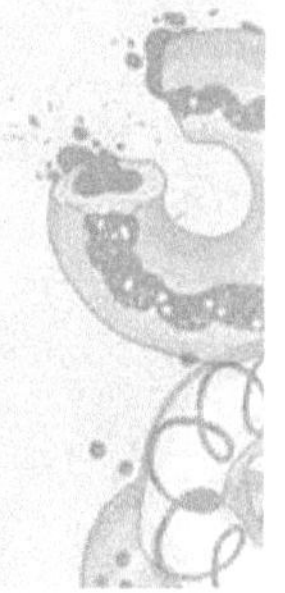

"A *man who*
Undervalues
Himself
Is sure to be a
Victim of
*Depression.***"** *!!!!!!!!!!!!!!!!!*

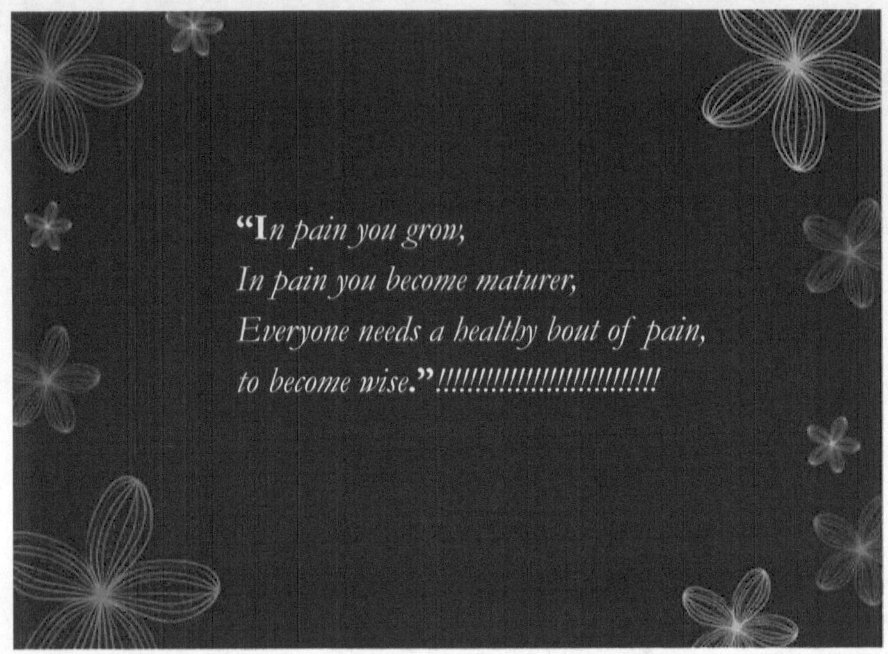

*"**I**n a man*
The only worthwhile driving force is
Passion!!!!!!!!!!!!!!!!
It just makes you run
For a passionate man
Success is an inherent
manifestation."!!!!!!!!!!!!!!!!!!!

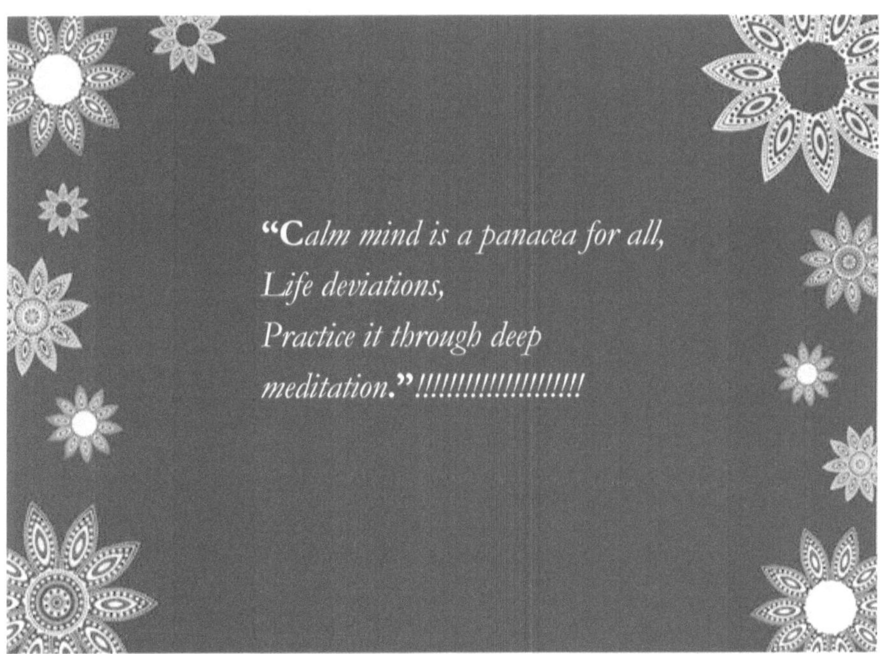
"Calm mind is a panacea for all,
Life deviations,
Practice it through deep
meditation."!!!!!!!!!!!!!!!!!!!!!

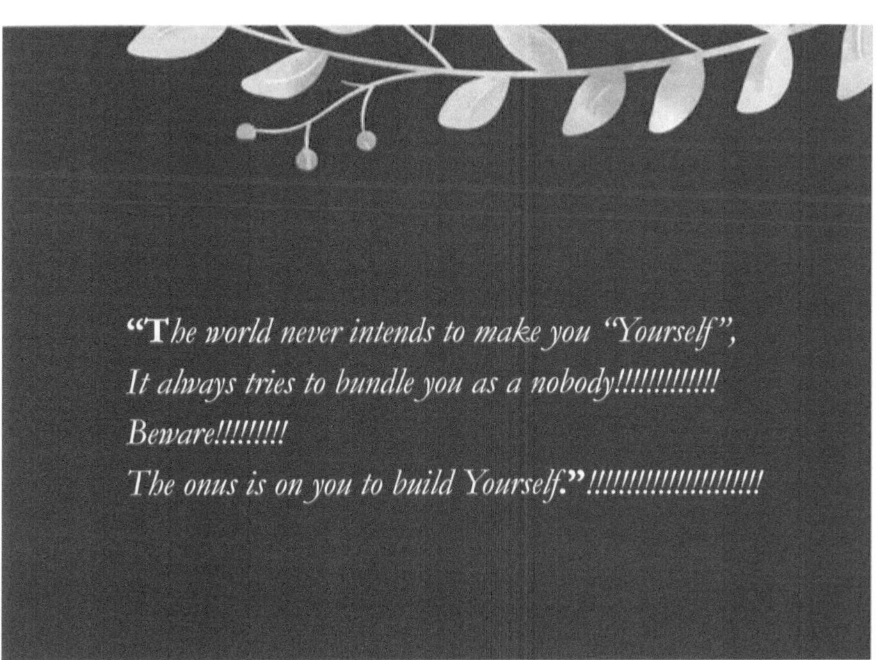
"The world never intends to make you "Yourself",
It always tries to bundle you as a nobody!!!!!!!!!!!!!!
Beware!!!!!!!!!
The onus is on you to build Yourself."!!!!!!!!!!!!!!!!!!!!!!

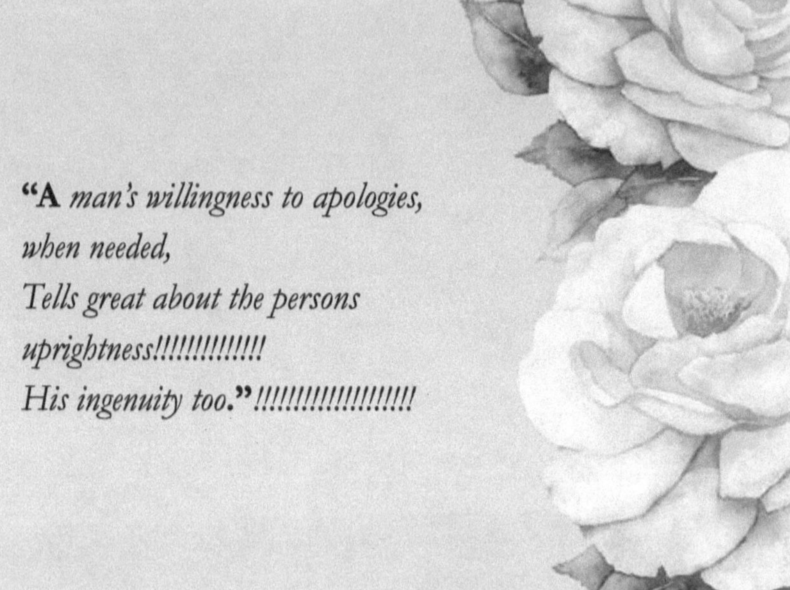
"A man's willingness to apologies,
when needed,
Tells great about the persons
uprightness!!!!!!!!!!!!!!
His ingenuity too."!!!!!!!!!!!!!!!!!!!!!

"It is more fortunate to be in someone's heart,
Rather than being in one's mind."!!!!!!!!!!!!!!!!!!.......

"E*xhibit your flaws prominently........*
Firstly it makes you honest and transparent!!!!!!!!!!!!!!!!
Secondly, your adversaries will loose you in earnest."!!!!!!!

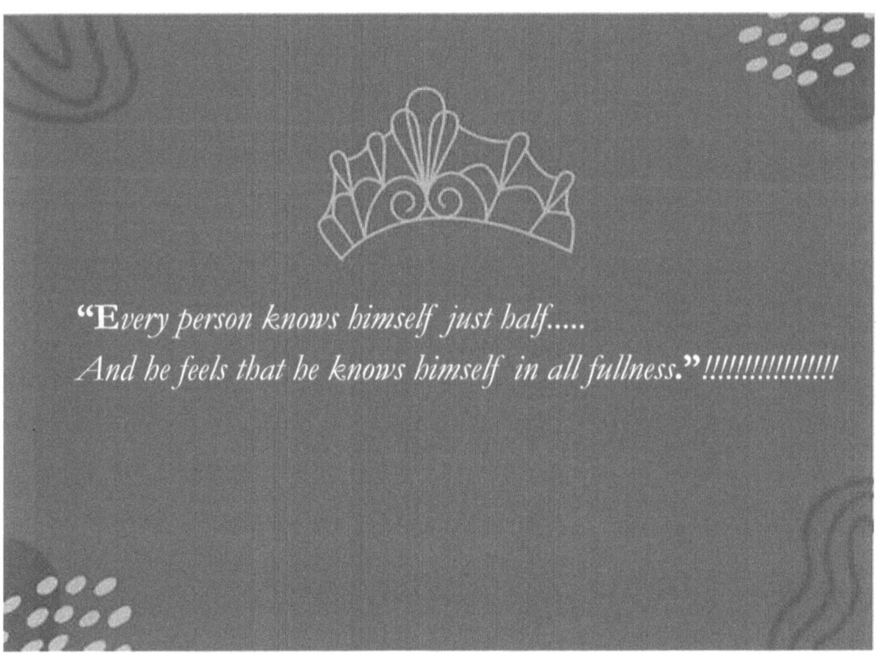

"The more you listen,
The more you observe,
The more integral will you become."!!!!!!!!!!!!!!!

"When you believes in yourself,
You manifest an assurance of self love."!!!!!!!!!!!!!!!

*“**I**n this world, only the weak loves everybody,*
A strong willed man has his way of loving,
Which more or less, is
attitudinal.”!!!!!!!!!!!!!!!!!!!!!

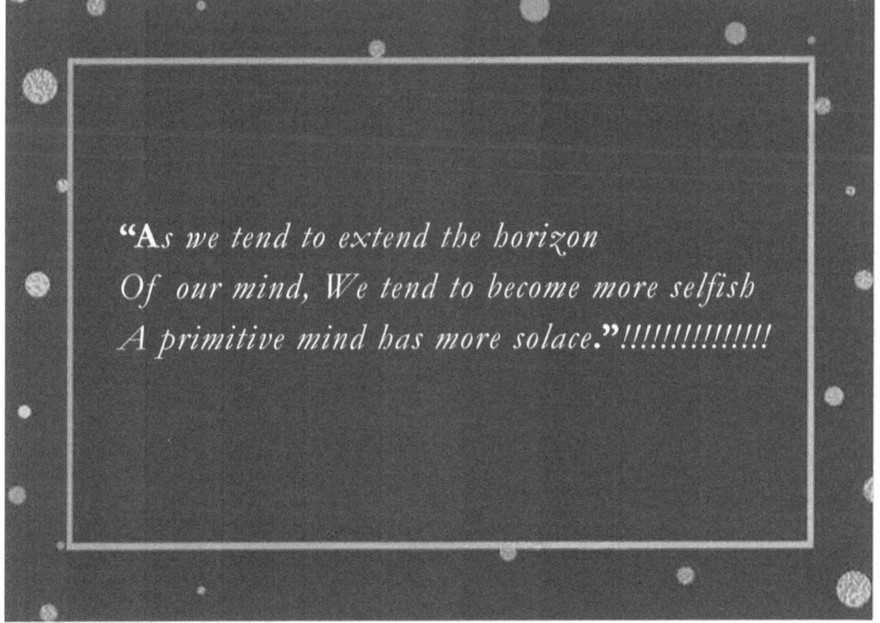

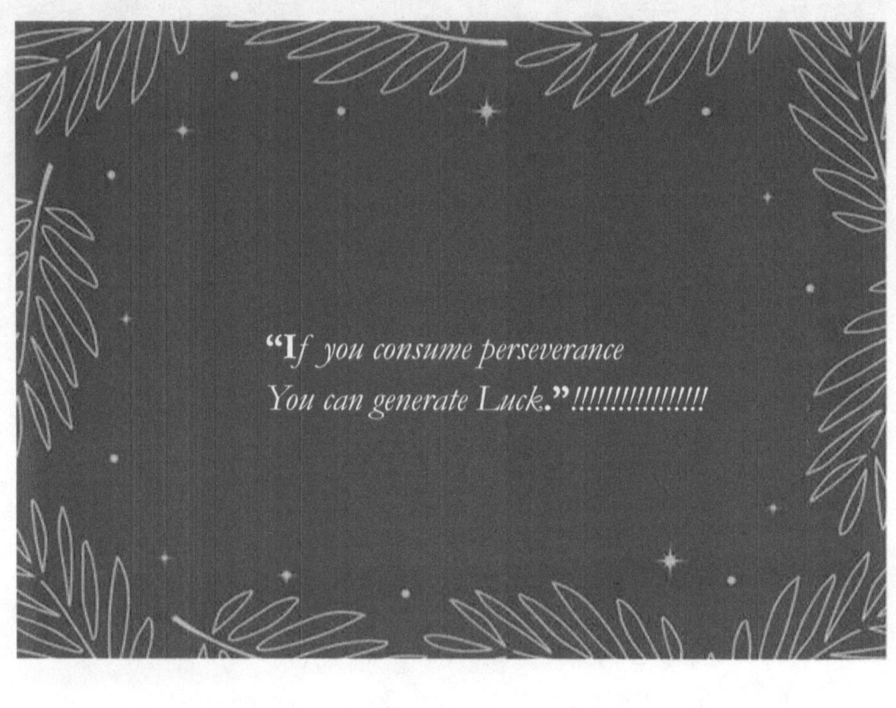

"Never be too possessive of your Respect............
Your respect is safe until you bungle with it.......
You are the fulcrum of your respect."!!!!!!!!!!!!!!!!!!!!!

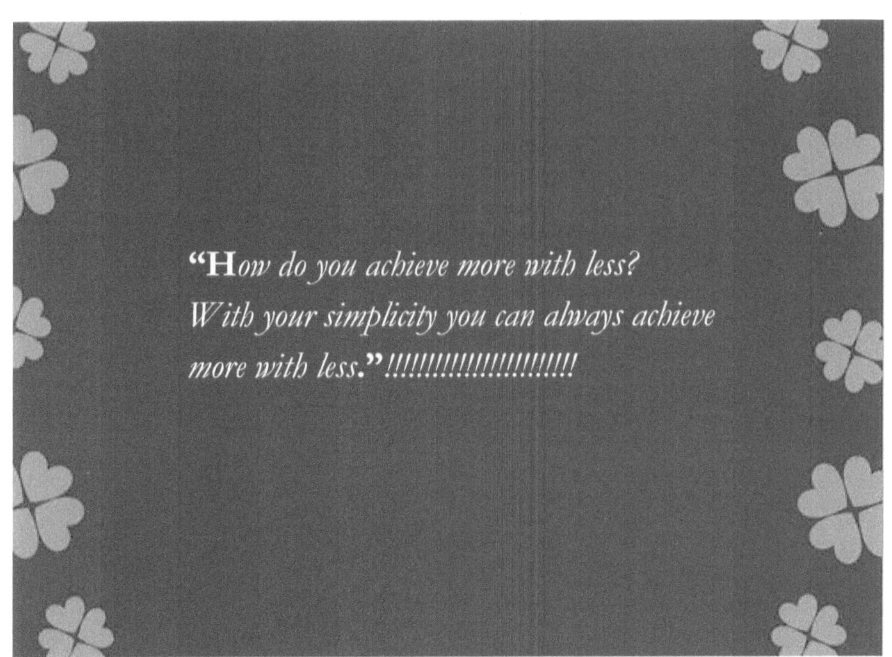
"How do you achieve more with less?
With your simplicity you can always achieve
more with less."!!!!!!!!!!!!!!!!!!!!!!!!

"Learn from your mistakes...................
Never waste them."!!!!!!!!!!!!!!!!!

"**T***o transform the world,*
We need humility, perseverance and trust." !!!!!!!!!!!!!!!!!!!!!!

"**P***eople regret, Why-*
1. They never try to discover themselves!!!!!!!!!!!!
2. They are disdainful of Empathy!!!!!!!!!!!!
3. They are prisoners of their Dislikes!!!!!!!!!!!!
4. They never value Time!!!!!!!!!!!!
5. They don't have a healthy family bonding." !!!!!!!!!!!!

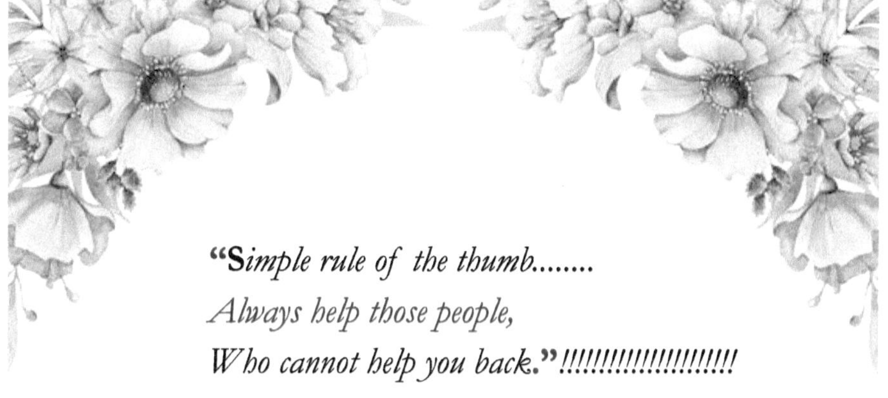

"**S***imple rule of the thumb........*
Always help those people,
Who cannot help you back."!!!!!!!!!!!!!!!!!!!!!!

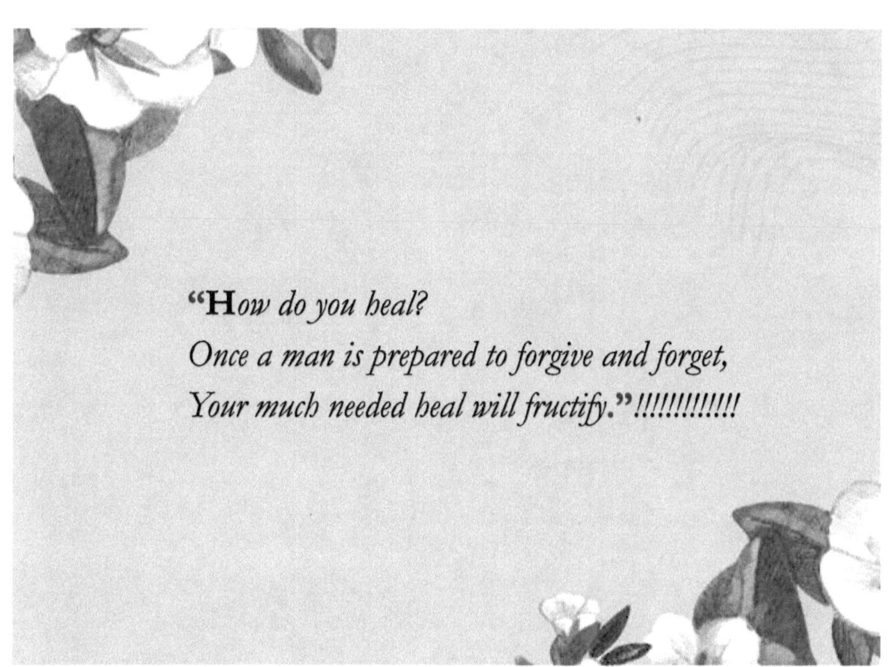

"**H***ow do you heal?*
Once a man is prepared to forgive and forget,
Your much needed heal will fructify."!!!!!!!!!!!!!

"Willpower and focused determination,
With a tinge of perseverance
Will lead you anywhere you wish to go." !!!!!!!!!!!!!

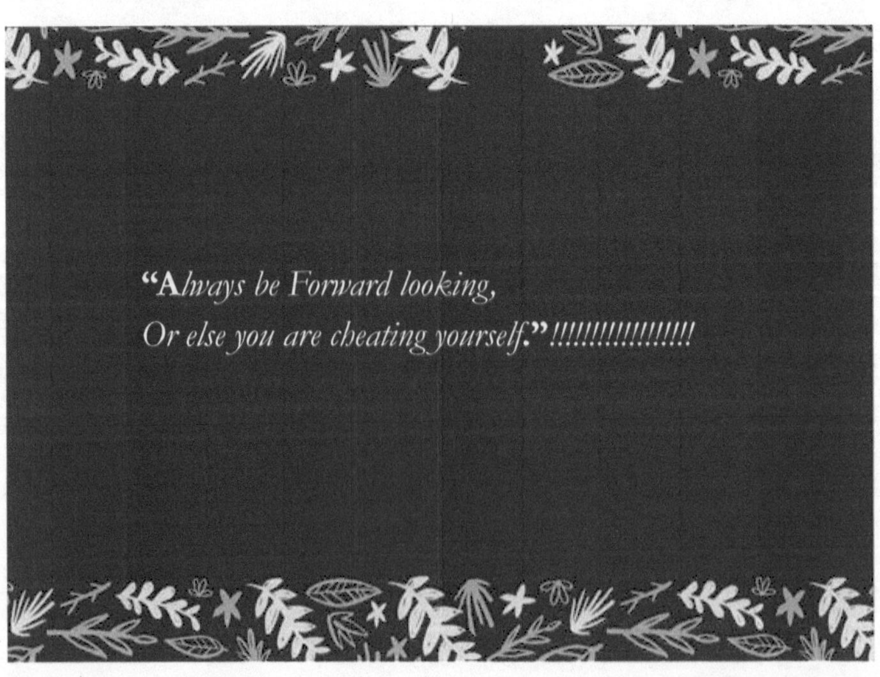
"Always be Forward looking,
Or else you are cheating yourself." !!!!!!!!!!!!!!!!!

*"**A**lways listen to others, but*
Be cautious.........
Never lend your ears." !!!!!!!!!!!!!!!!!!!!!!!!!

*"**I**f anybody treats you badly,*
Never react..................
By it you grow wiser and stronger." !!!!!!!!!!!!!!!

"**M***an is seen in this age in a constantly chasing mode……….. The unending saga of consumerism.*" !!!!!!!!!!!!!!!!!!!!!

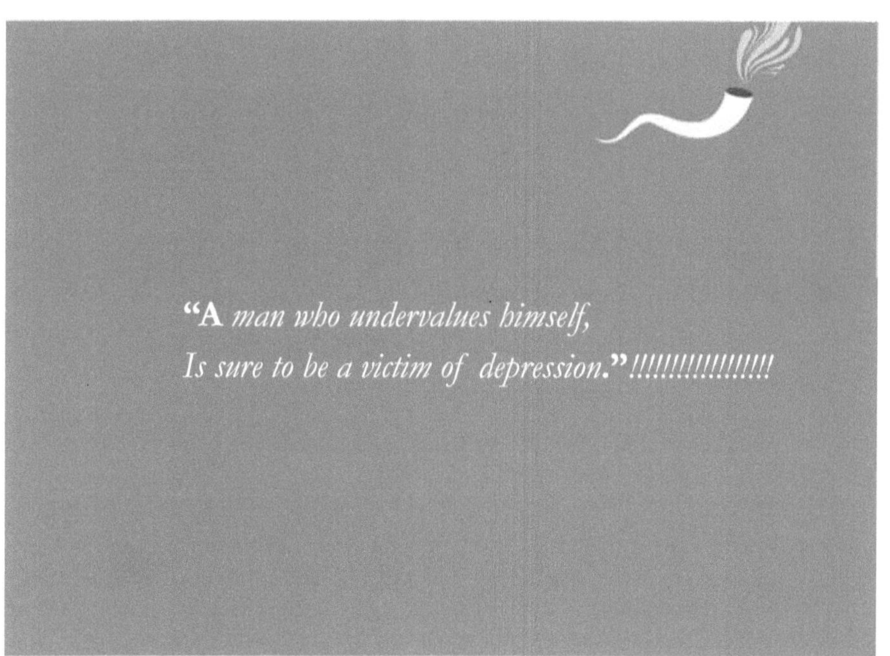

“**A** *man who undervalues himself,*
Is sure to be a victim of depression.”!!!!!!!!!!!!!!!!!!

“**N***ever wait for your moment,*
Create one for yourself.”!!!!!!!!!!!!!!!!!!!

"**M***an is at the helm of,*
God's creation!!!!!!!!!!!!!!!!!!!!!
Before Man, God might have been an
impossibility."!!!!!!!!!!!!!!!!!!!!!!!!!!!!!!!!!

"**I***f you are an emancipator,*
Only then you become a passionate Giver."!!!!!!!!!!!!!!!!!!!!!!!!!!

*“**R**esilience is one of the most,*
Arduous workouts
That man should practice.” !!!!!!!!!!!!!!!

*“**W**hen you cannot see yourself, you. Fail...........*
When you can see yourself, you succeed.” !!!!!!!!!!!!!!

"**A** *man with too many,*
And too frequent excuses..............
Becomes stationary."*!!!!!!!!!!!!!!!!!!*

"**I***ntegrity is behavioural*
Give impetus to your behaviour
And integrity will fall in line."*!!!!!!!!!!!!!!!!!!!!!!!!!!*

“F*ortune favours the brave*
Risking rewires your fortunes.” *!!!!!!!!!!*

“A *kind mind is never known for the looks.*” *!!!!!!!!!!!!!!!!!!!*

***"T**he parameter of a good man is, the essentiality.....,*
He shouldn't be in the good books of everyone,
He should, necessarily be hated by a few too."!!!!!!!!!!!!!!!!

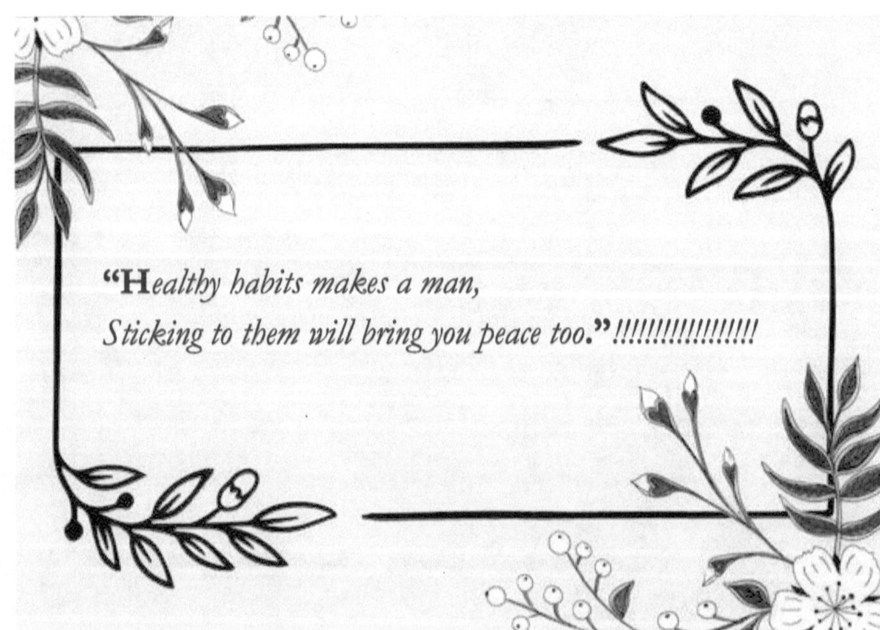

***"H**ealthy habits makes a man,*
Sticking to them will bring you peace too."!!!!!!!!!!!!!!!!!!

“A successful man can be happy,
But a happy man may not necessarily be
successful.” !!!!!!!!!!!!!!!!

“People good at heart,
Are invariably not a success.” !!!!!!!!!!!!!!!!!!

***“A**lways project people,*
Better than yourself.” !!!!!!!!!!!!!!!!!

***“A** gentle soul always have,*
A troubled conscience.” !!!!!!!!!!!!!!!!!

*“**B**rave never worry for tomorrow,*
They only work for the present.” !!!!!!!!!!!!!!!!!!!!

*“**T**he greatest battles we fight,*
Are the battles fought lonely.” !!!!!!!!!!!!!!!!!!

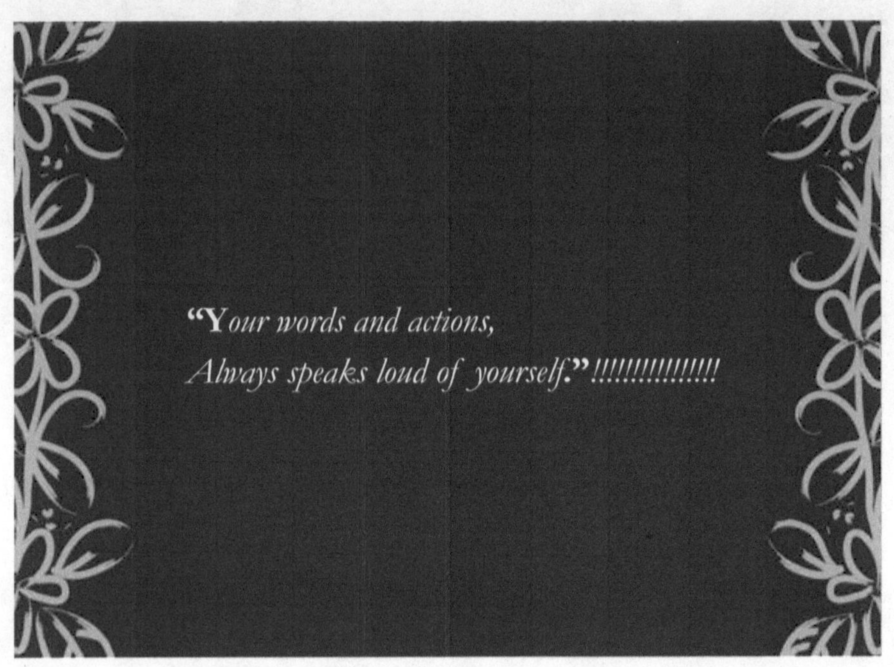
"Your words and actions,
Always speaks loud of yourself."!!!!!!!!!!!!!!!!

"Everyone is fighting a battle,
Some in bedroom,
Some in battlefield."!!!!!!!!!!!!!!!!!!!!

*"**M**an is too unfortunate,*
He never tries to live up with his beliefs." !!!!!!!!!!!!!!!!!!!

*"**W**hy men get delayed success?*
He is late in getting lessons from his failures." !!!!!!!!!!!!!!

"Never pit a loyal person against a wall,
With your doubting behaviour." !!!!!!!!!!!!!!!!!!

"People who are sincere on their front foot,
May necessarily not be sincere upon their backfoot." !!!!!!!!!!!!!!!!!!

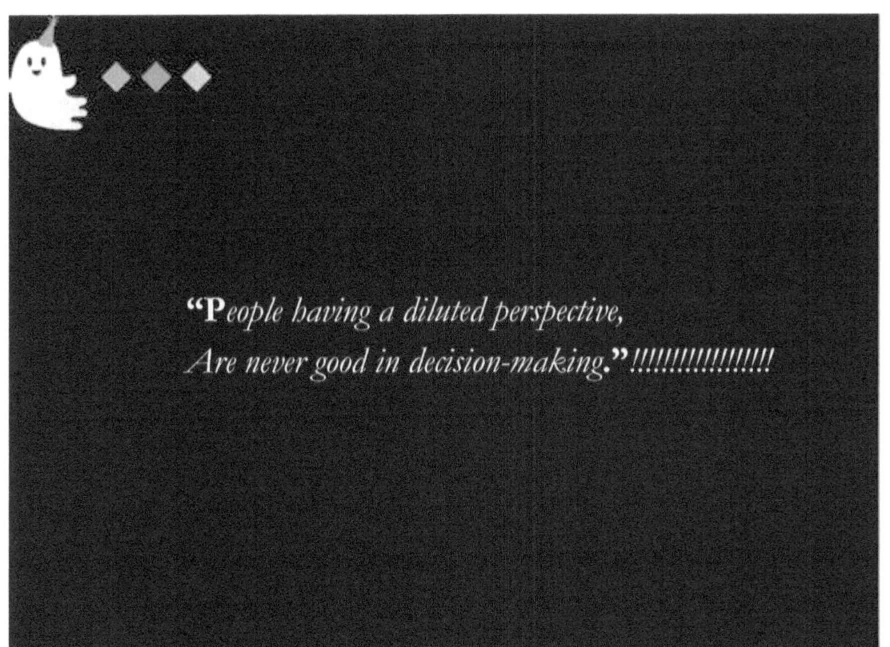
“People having a diluted perspective,
Are never good in decision-making.”!!!!!!!!!!!!!!!!!!

“Judging is the most favourites of people’s
pastimes across.”!!!!!!!!!!!!!!!!!!!!

"Reading is,
Making yourself equip to face the world,
Face yourself too."!!!!!!!!!!!!!!

"Self-control gives discipline,
Right thinking gives better behaviour,
And calmness of mind gives
clarity."!!!!!!!!!!!!!!!!!!

*“**O**nce you become adamant with your self-discovery, You need two things!!!!!!!!!!!!!!!!!!
You should be ruthless and hard with yourself,
You should draw yourself towards complete simplicity, With trust and integrity as pillars.”!!!!!!!!!!!!!!!!!!*

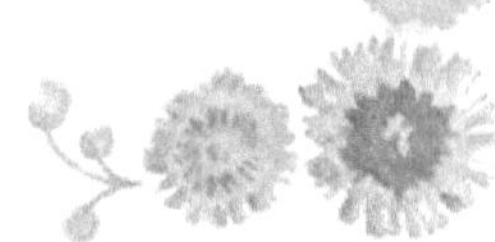

*“**E**nough is never enough,
It is a sea of never ending wish-list.........
The greatest infirmity which a man has.”!!!!!!!!!!!!!!!!!!*

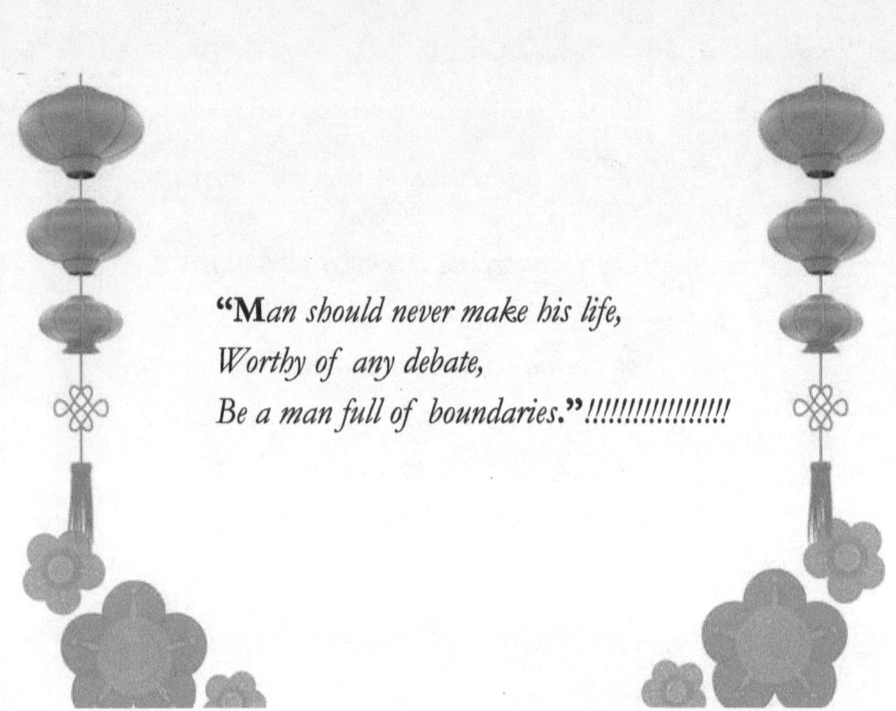

"**M***an should never make his life,*
Worthy of any debate,
Be a man full of boundaries." !!!!!!!!!!!!!!!!!!!

"**A***nimals can be loyal to man,*
But man being loyal to animals is a doubtful preposition." !!!!!!!!!!!!!!!!!

*"**S**trong people love silence,*
Weak people love words,
Valiant ones love actions."!!!!!!!!!!!!!!!!

*"**P**eople are in a bad habit of burying people fast...............*
The lesser their self-interest, the faster your burial."!!!!!!!!!!!!!!!!!!

"**A** *pauper is defined by his patience,*
A wealthy man is there with his attitude." !!!!!!!!!!!!!!!!!!

"**A** *responsible man is,*
Always a successful man." !!!!!!!!!!!!!!!!!!

"**H***umans cannot teach humanity,*
For they are not humil."!!!!!!!!!!!!!!!!!!

"**N***ever incarnate anything as impossible......*
Even for fools, everything is possible."!!!!!!!!!!!!!!!!!!

"**M***an is not simplistic,*
*He musters great courage in Trusting God.***"** !!!!!!!!!!!!!!

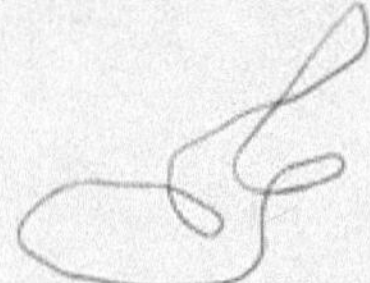

"**L***earn to move with right people,*
Although it is also said that right people come into your Life,
*Only if you are destined.***"** !!!!!!!!!!!!!??????????????

"**M***an's life is illusiory,*
The very reason of man's stresses, problems, and
the Incoming insecurities."!!!!!!!!!!!!!!!!!!

"**M***ind limits man's aspirations.......*
But his tenacity can overrule,
Minds neurons can electrify his ambitions."!!!!!!!!!!!!!!

“A *man always loves a person,*
Who calls him by his name.” !!!!!!!!!!!!!!!!!!

“N*ever be more interested,*
Always try to become more interesting,
You become vibrant.” !!!!!!!!!!!!!!!

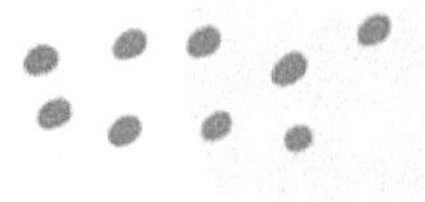

*“**W**hat we carry inside us,*
Is the antithesis of what we see outside.” !!!!!!!!!!!!!!!!!!

*“**Y**our heart and soul are your*
heavyweights.......
Human mind always disobeys
them.” !!!!!!!!!!!!!!!!!!!!!!

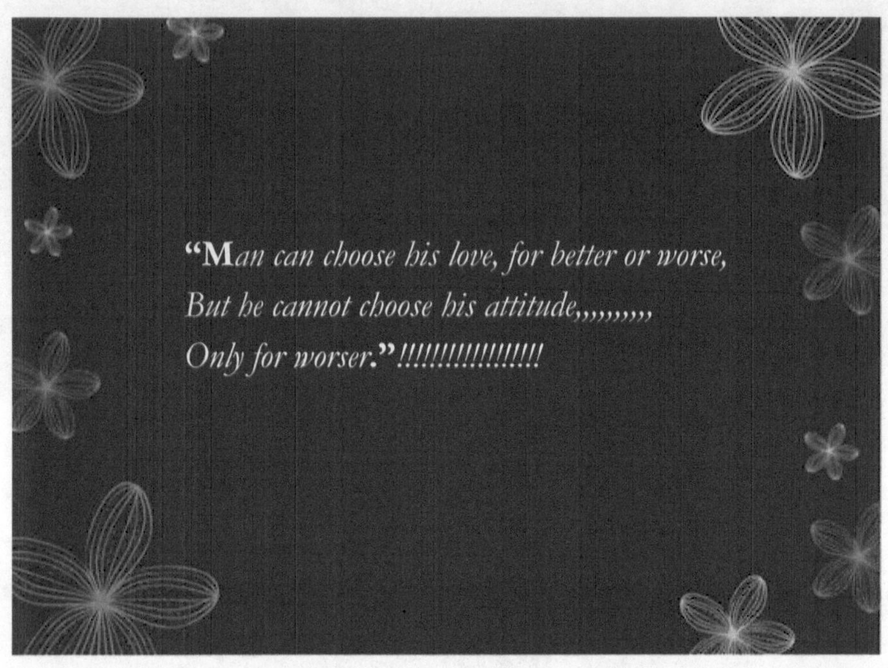
"Man can choose his love, for better or worse,
But he cannot choose his attitude,,,,,,,,,,
Only for worser."!!!!!!!!!!!!!!!!!!

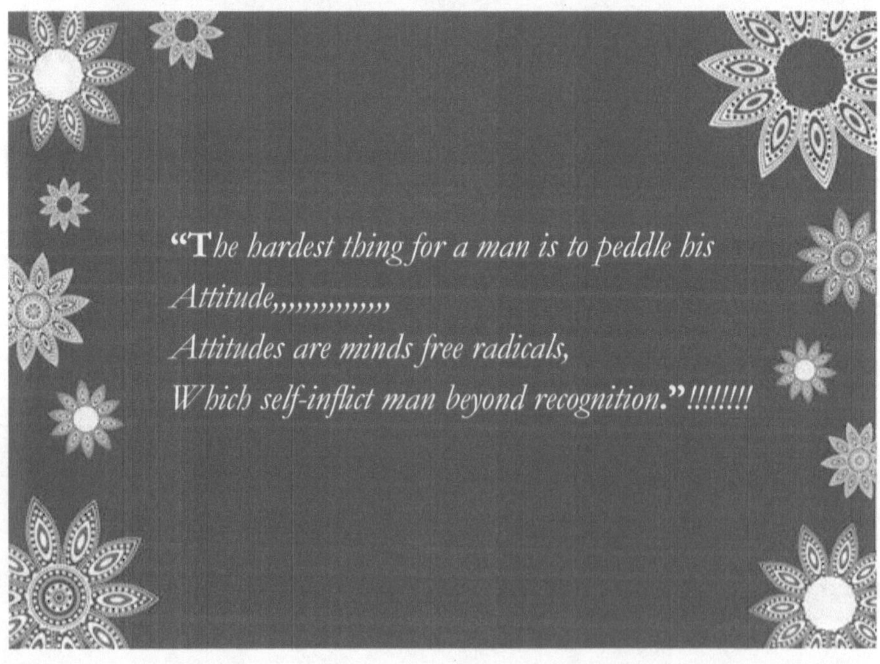
"The hardest thing for a man is to peddle his
Attitude,,,,,,,,,,,,,,,
Attitudes are minds free radicals,
Which self-inflict man beyond recognition."!!!!!!!!

*"**B**ravery is an attitude,*
A fearful person can also be brave..........
Provided he is not having any mental ailment." !!!!!!!!!!!!

Woman

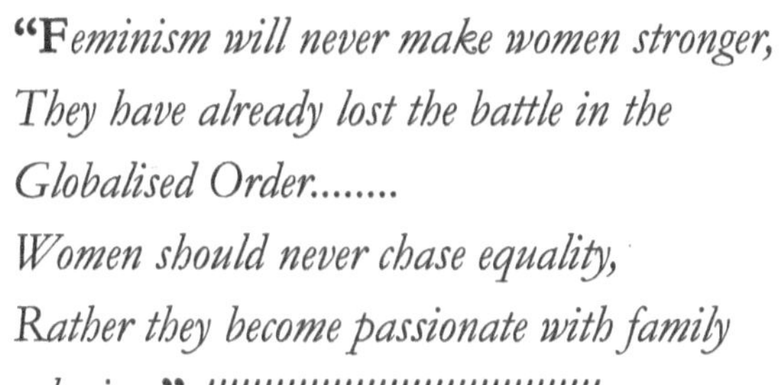
"Feminism will never make women stronger,
They have already lost the battle in the
Globalised Order........
Women should never chase equality,
Rather they become passionate with family
cohesion." !!!!!!!!!!!!!!!!!!!!!!!!!!!!!!!!!!!!!

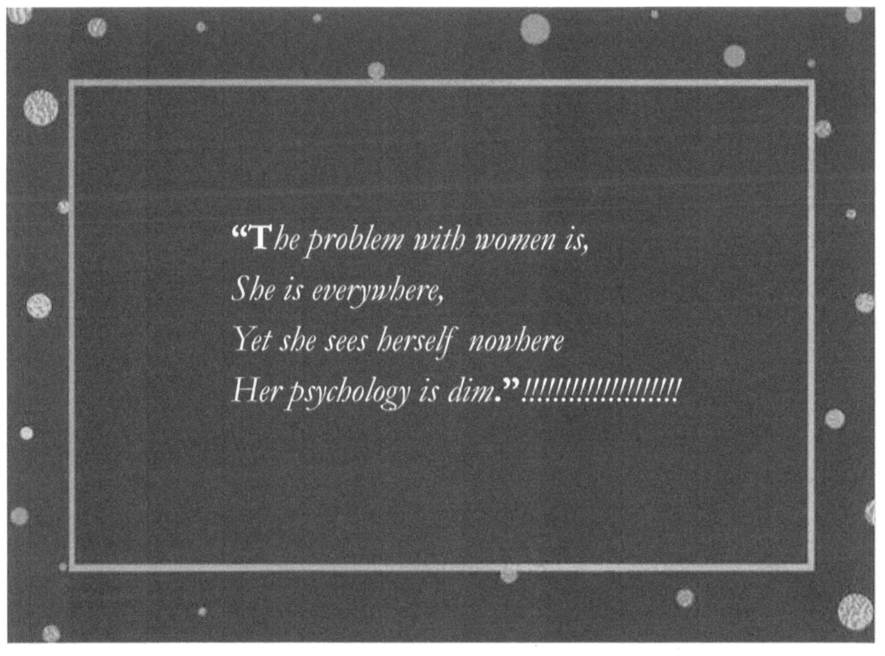
"The problem with women is,
She is everywhere,
Yet she sees herself nowhere
Her psychology is dim."!!!!!!!!!!!!!!!!!!!!

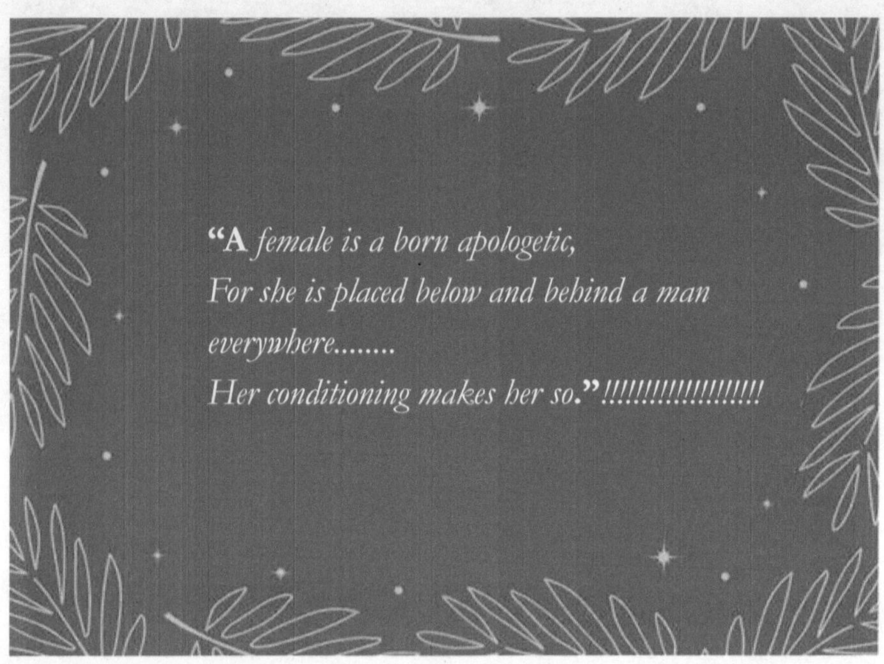

“W*omen cannot be happy,*
For they are loaded with
responsibilities,
The irony is that men are weak
in owing
Responsibilities.”!!!!!!!!!!!!!!!!!!!!

"**A** *Woman in good chemistry with her mother..............*
Will never prove to be a reliable life-partner."!!!!!!!!!!!!!!!

"**W***omen are psychologically infirm..........*
They never say what they mean.......,
They always do what they feel........
And this is a dangerous predicament for any social Chemistry."!!!!!!!!!!!!!!!!!!!!!!!!!!

"A smiling woman can even sell mud............
Such is the aura of a her smile."!!!!!!!!!!!!!!!!!!!!

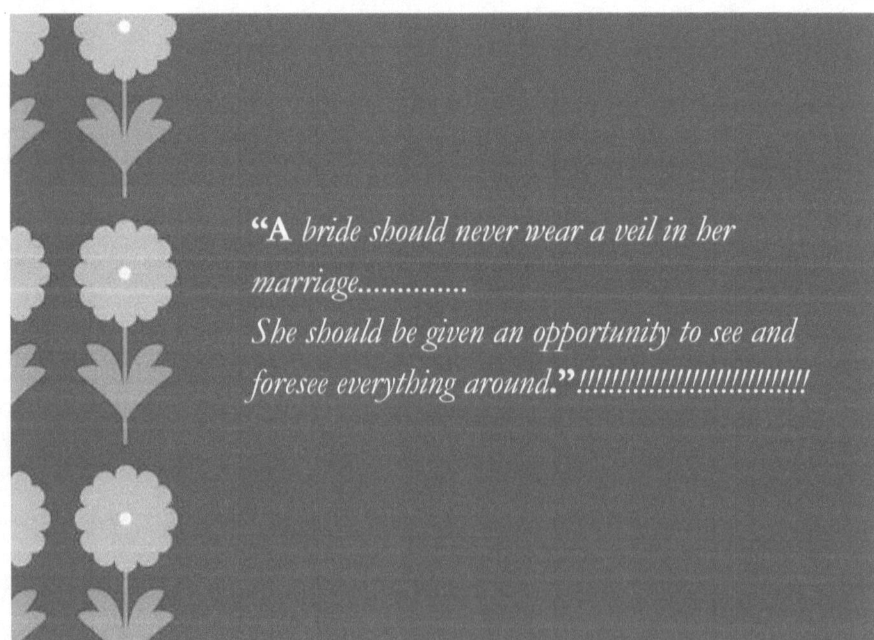
"A bride should never wear a veil in her marriage..............
She should be given an opportunity to see and foresee everything around."!!!!!!!!!!!!!!!!!!!!!!!!!!!!!!

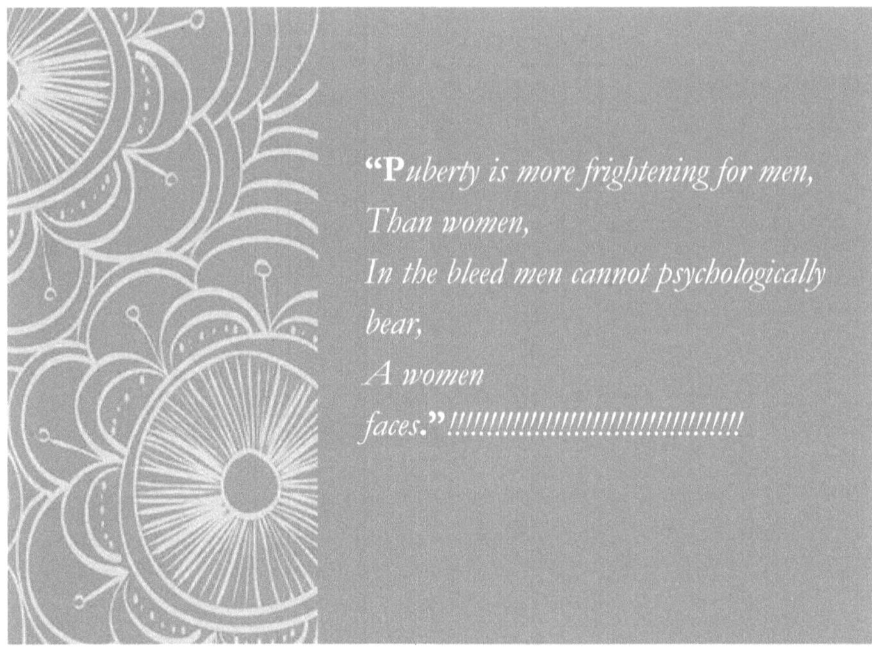
"Puberty is more frightening for men,
Than women,
In the bleed men cannot psychologically
bear,
A women
faces."!!

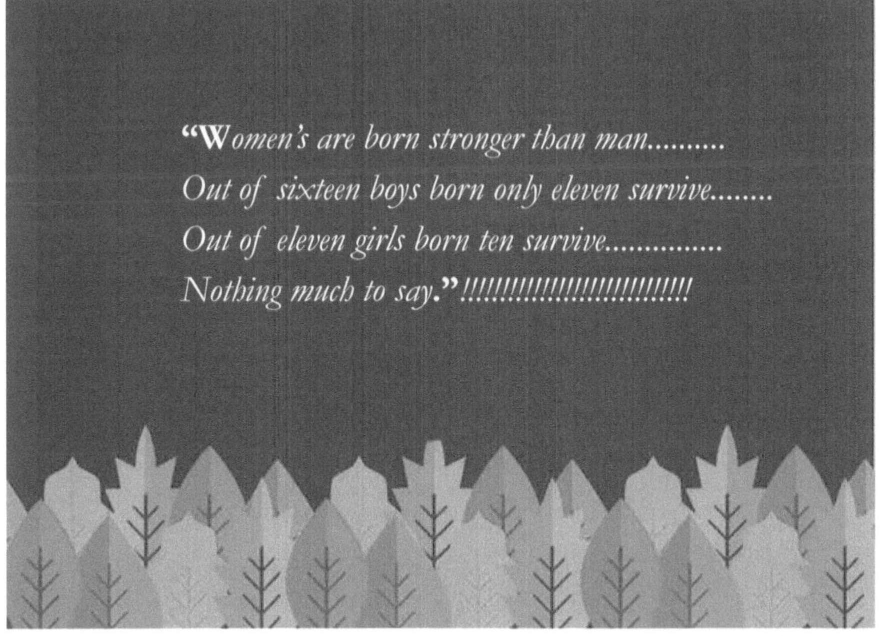
"Women's are born stronger than man..........
Out of sixteen boys born only eleven survive........
Out of eleven girls born ten survive..............
Nothing much to say."!!!!!!!!!!!!!!!!!!!!!!!!!!!!!!!!

"**T***he whole energies of our Age,*
Is being misused in pampering women."!!!!!!!!!!!!!!!

"**A** *girl-child cannot grow to complete maturity,*
If she has missed the shadow of her father in childhood."!!!!!!!!!!!!!!!!!!!!!!!!!

*"**I**f you want your man to love you for a lifetime,
Feed him on... satiating fresh cooked food,
If you want a Women to love for you for a
lifetime, give her a feeling of wholesome sense of
security."!!!!!!!!!!!!!!!!*

*"**W**hy aren't women visionary??????
Their hormonal metaphysics disturbs
their concentration!!!!!!!!!!.
Their visionary aptitude
stops within the precincts of
sexuality."!!!!!!!!!!!!!!!!!!!!!!!!!!!!!!!!!!!!*

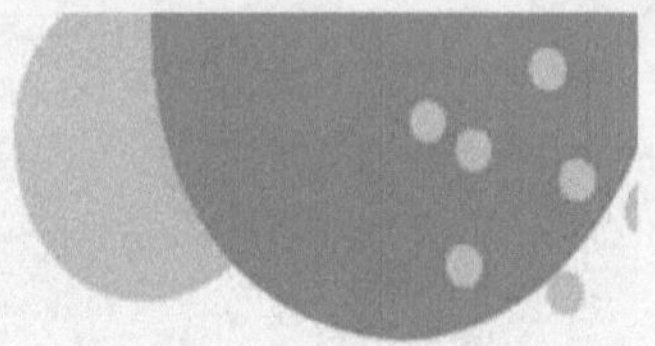

"**T***he premium for looking beautiful*
Is draining women out." !!!!!!!!!!!!!!!

"**W***omen are a matrix of amazement.*" !!!!!!!!!!!!!!!!!!!!!!

“A *woman is grateful only once, for the first time...........*
In the birth of her new born........
Her whole person vibrates in fine tune with the Grace of
‘Him’.” !!!!!!!!!!!!!!!!!!!!!!!!!!!!!!!!!

“W*omen are revered across Cultures*
In all times,
And times to come.” !!!!!!!!!!!!!!!!!!!!!!!!!!!

"Women symbolises poise,
The only inherent virtue on earth."!!!!!!!!!!

"Women lack an exuberant mindset,
They have a closeted aura."!!!!!!!!!!!!!!!!!!!!!!!!!

"**W***omen are at the apex of creations,*
Why should be they mindful of small parities?" !!!!!!!!!!!

"**S***top judging women*
Your women will become your greatest
Ally." !!!!!!!!!!!!!!!!

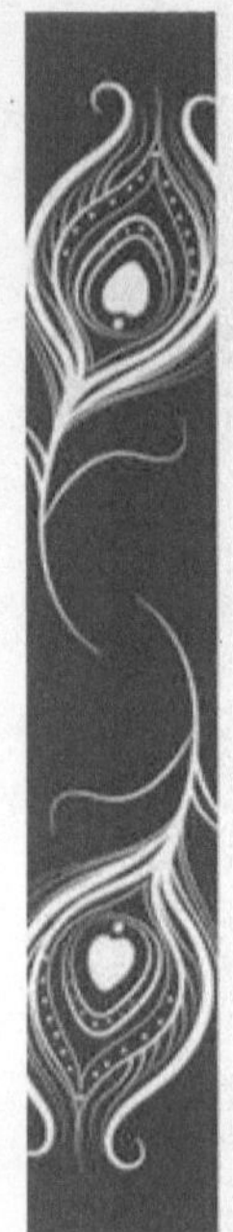

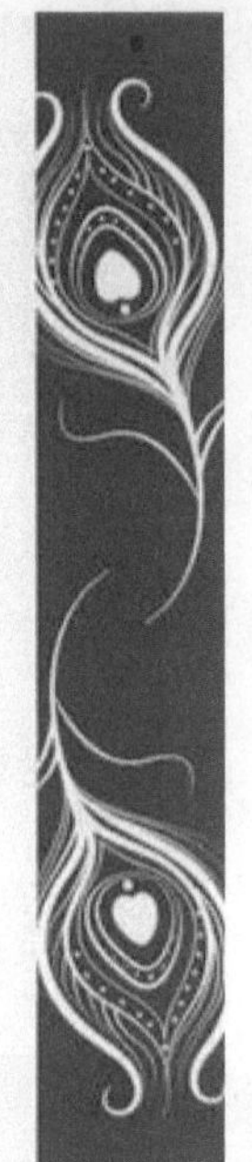

*"Jingo Womanhood,
Has pushed man in the most secluded
vulnerability."* !!!!!!!!!!!!!!!!!

*"Women are prejudices fighting machine
Man has put her so."* !!!!!!!!!!!!!!!!!!!!!!!!!

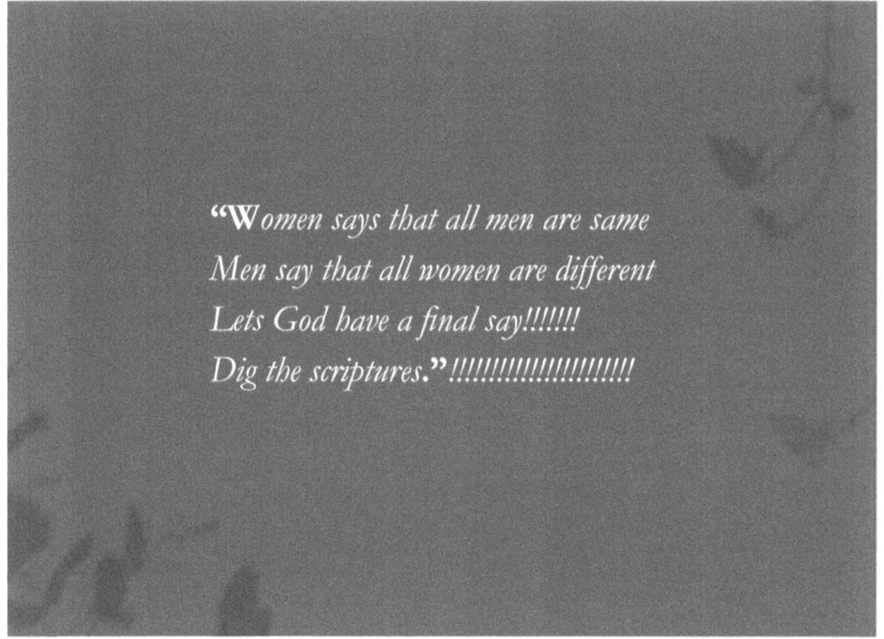

"I*n human ageing progression,*
A man is better placed than a woman,
Old age is more painful for a woman than a man."!!!!!!!!!

*“**I**f a female is not pretty,*
She incarnates a guilt.” !!!!!!!!!!!!!!

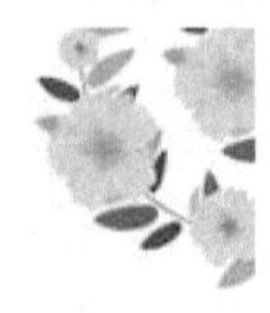

*“**H**eels stupidifys a women*
Instead of giving a height,
It makes her diminutive.” !!!!!!!!!!!!!!!!!!!!

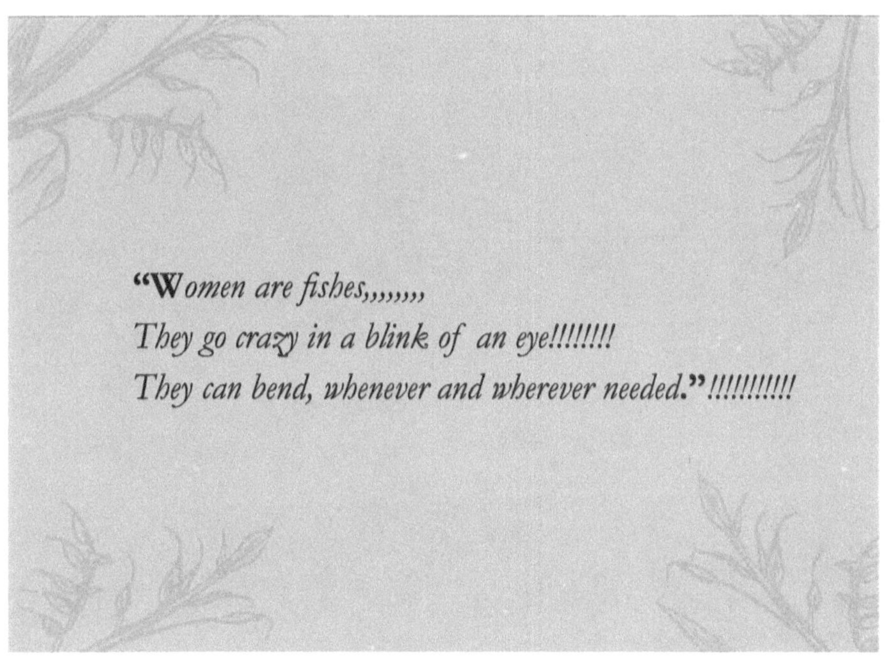

*"**W**omen are fishes,,,,,,,,,*
They go crazy in a blink of an eye!!!!!!!!
They can bend, whenever and wherever needed."!!!!!!!!!!

*"**F**or a woman, age isn't just a number*
It is an pivotal axis for her well
being."!!!!!!!!!!!!!!!!

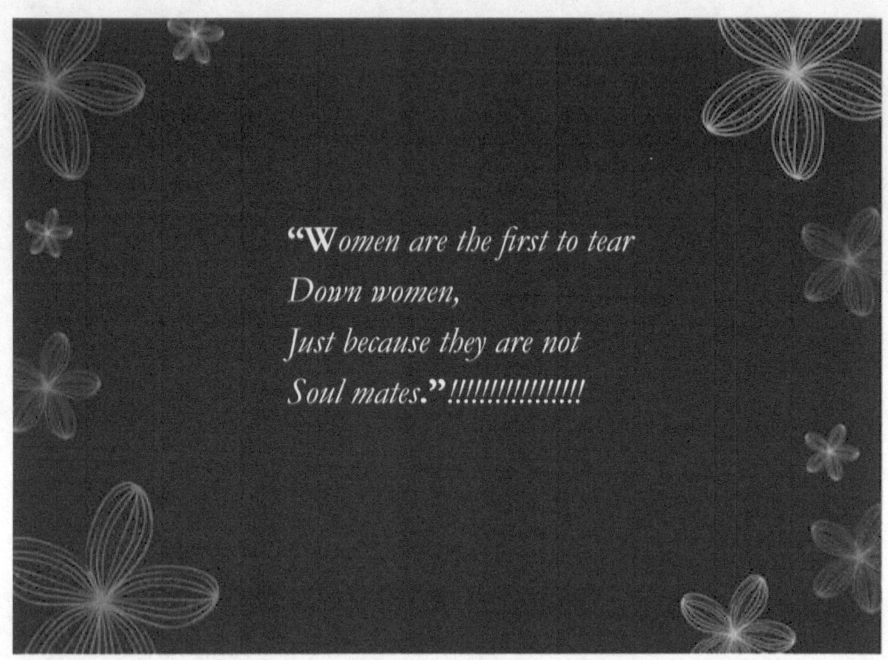
"Women are the first to tear
Down women,
Just because they are not
Soul mates."!!!!!!!!!!!!!!!!

"Sickness for women,
Is punishment."!!!!!!!!!!!!!!!!!!!!!!

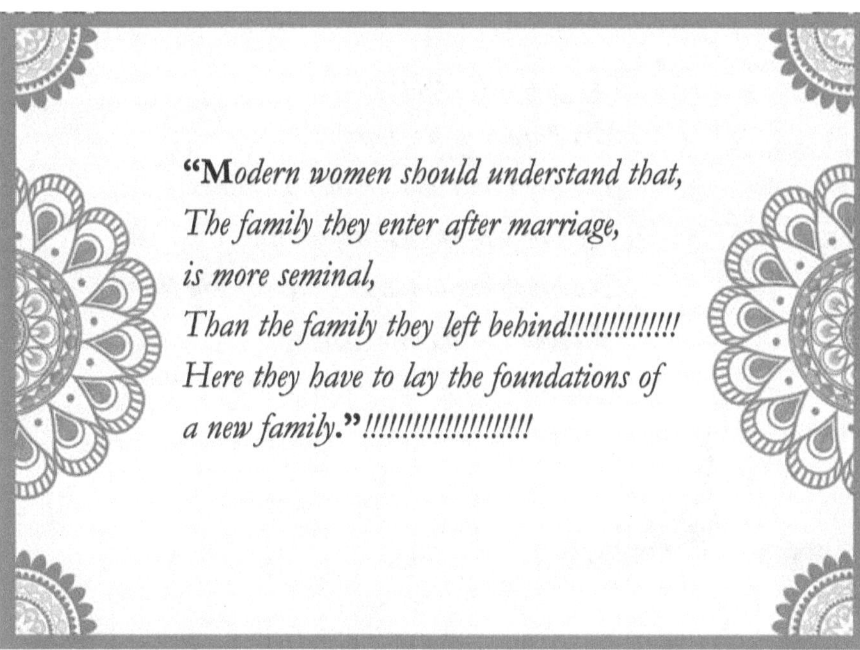
"Modern women should understand that,
The family they enter after marriage,
is more seminal,
Than the family they left behind!!!!!!!!!!!!!!
Here they have to lay the foundations of
a new family." !!!!!!!!!!!!!!!!!!!!!

"Dads have become
"Relics"!!!!!!!!!!!!
Women are lubricants, through
which everything is grinded
There is a perceptible shift in
power equation." !!!!!!!!!!!!!!

"If you are a woman...
You have to work harder
You are under the scanner of biases
Too much apologies are expected from you
Too much explanation waits for you there!
'Women', as a philosopher
Has said is the 'Second Sex'."!!!!!!!!!!!!!!!!!!!!

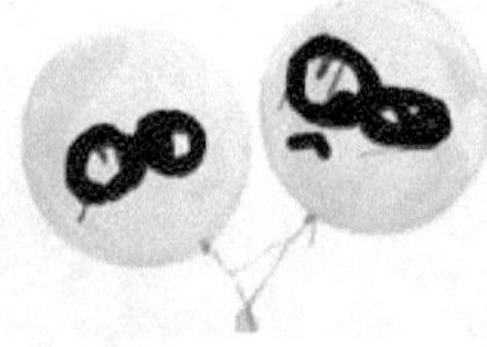

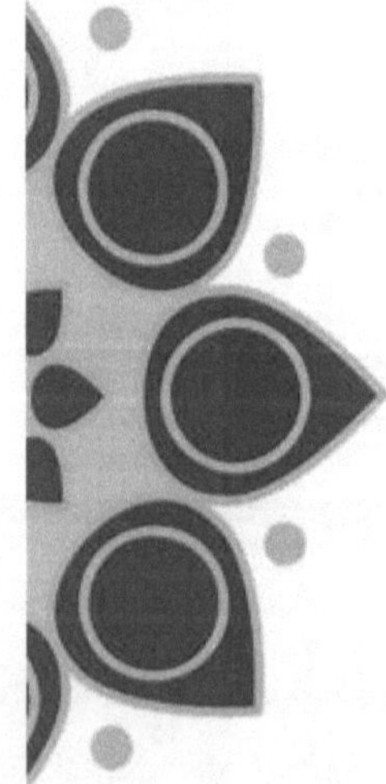

"Good looks, whether male or female............
Have an inherent attitudinal trajectory.........
More particularly females tend to project it in their workplace..........
They expect their work to be done by others......,
For they overvalue their good looks."!!!!!!!!!!!!!!!!!

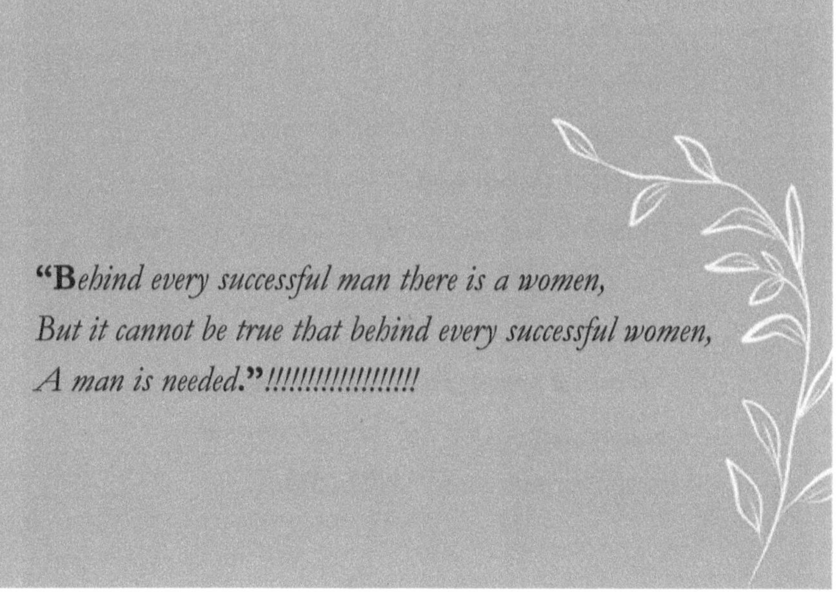

"**A***ll men cheat, some cheat better..........*
As for women, they are not lesser,
But their sting is deadlier."!!!!!!!!!!!!!!!!!!!!

"**I***s the world really in dire need for gender equality???????????*
A man cannot live without a women,
So too, a women cannot live without a man,
In such a case, we shouldn't clamour for equality,
But rather strive towards better cohesion towards each other!!!!!!!!!!!
Man and women shouldn't compete,
Rather they should fall for each other in a compassionate spirit."!!!!!!!!!!!!!!!!!!!!!!!!!

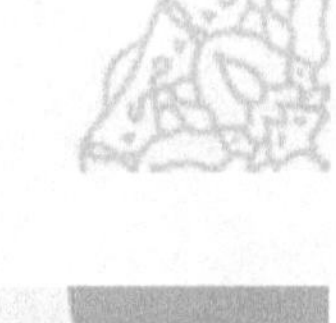

"**W***omen have more endurance, than men............*
Every month they come wrapped up in a pool of blood,
A journey wrought with pains."!!!!!!!!!!!!!!!!!!!!!!!!!!!!!!!

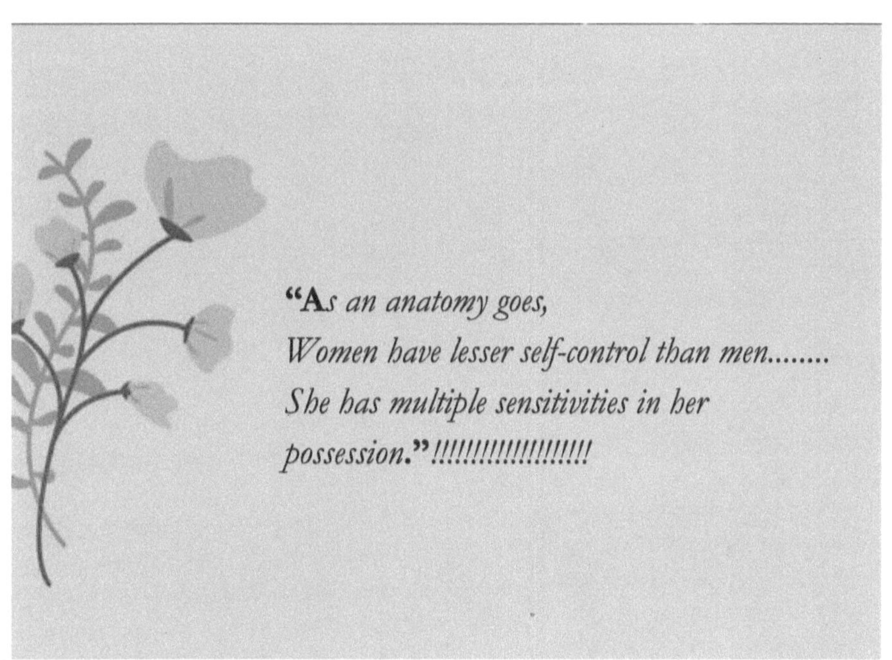
"As an anatomy goes,
Women have lesser self-control than men........
She has multiple sensitivities in her
possession."!!!!!!!!!!!!!!!!!!!!

God

God

"T*he more you trust God,*
The more you amass yourself."!!!!!!!!!!!!!!!!!!!!!!!!!!!!

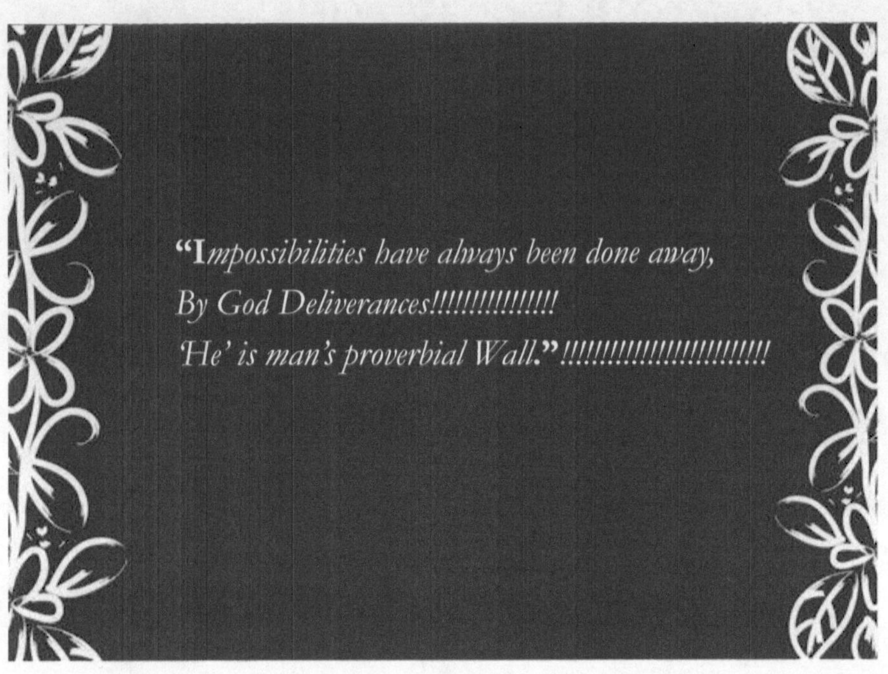

“**G***od builds man,*
Man should also rebuild himself.........
If he doesn’t, He will remain poor.”!!!!!!!!!!!!!!!!!!!!!!

*"**D**on't ever be in a hurry to manifest God,*
He will appear
And reappear,
When time ripens." !!!!!!!!!!!!!!!!!!!!!!!!!!!!!!

*"**T**rusting God has become necessary in these times,*
For man through his deeds has become a non-option." !!!!!!!!!!!!!!!!!!!!!!!!

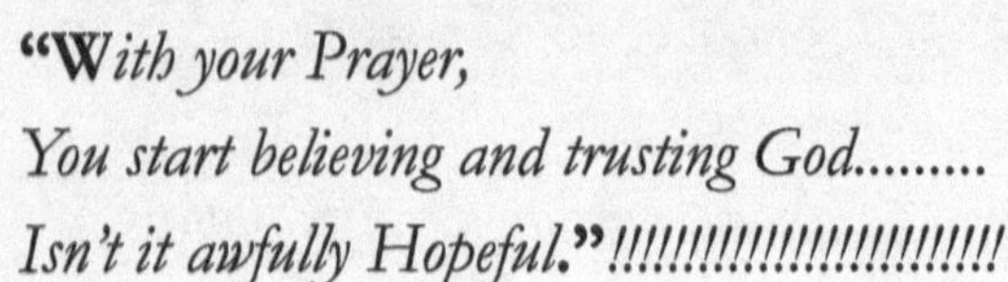
"With your Prayer,
You start believing and trusting God.........
Isn't it awfully Hopeful."!!!!!!!!!!!!!!!!!!!!!!!!!!

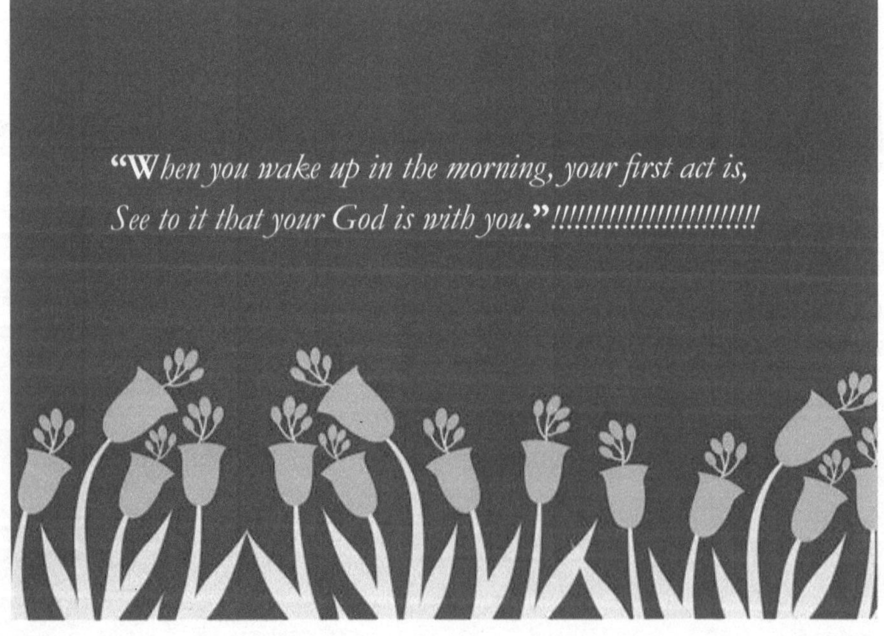
"When you wake up in the morning, your first act is,
See to it that your God is with you."!!!!!!!!!!!!!!!!!!!!!!!!!!

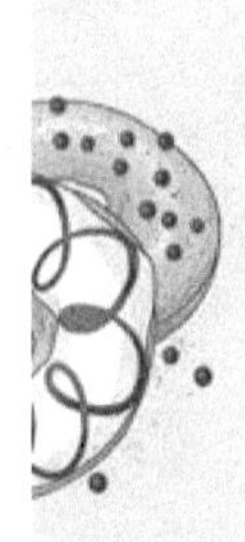

*"**A**dore" Hope",*
It is a one stop solution of all your
insecurities." !!!!!!!!!!!!!!!!!!!!

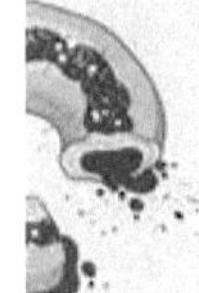

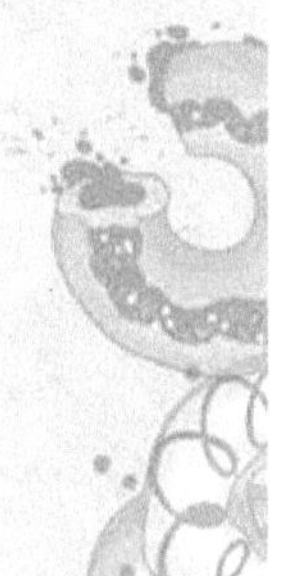

*"**R**egrets are your past fallacies,*
Make peace and mend with your surrender,
Before the Lord." !!!!!!!!!!!!!!!!!!!!!!!!!!!!!!!!!!!!

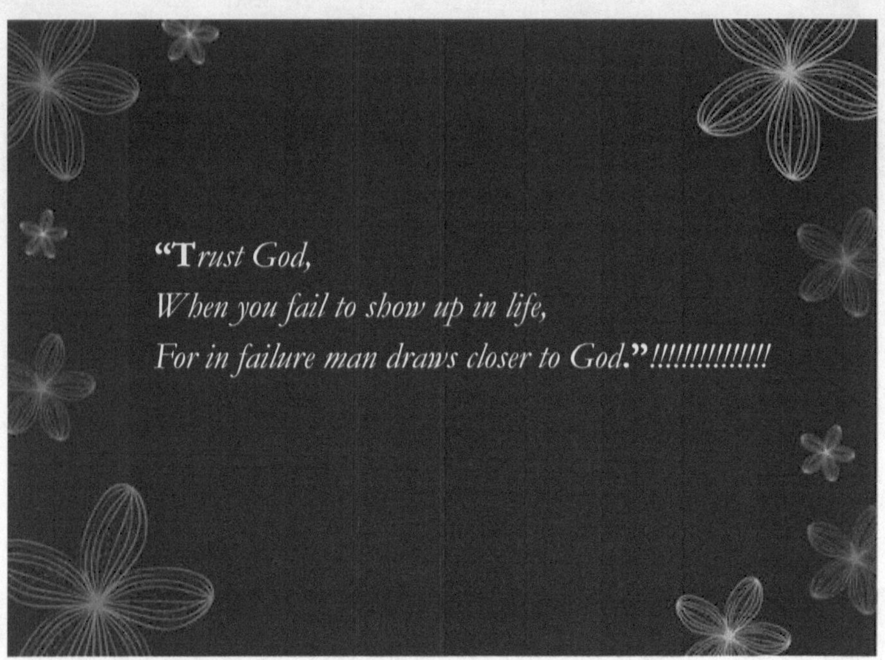

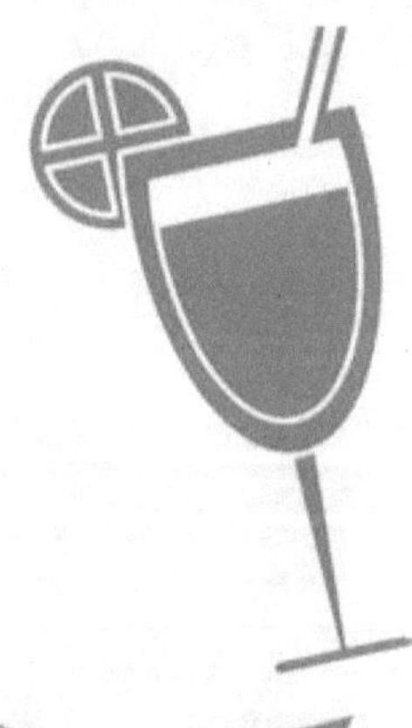

“**G***od has given man hope and future,*
To combat his curses.”!!!!!!!!!!!!!!!!!!!!!!!!!

"When rain falls!
Ensure that you get soaked first...
For you will be smelling God."!!!!!!!!!!!!

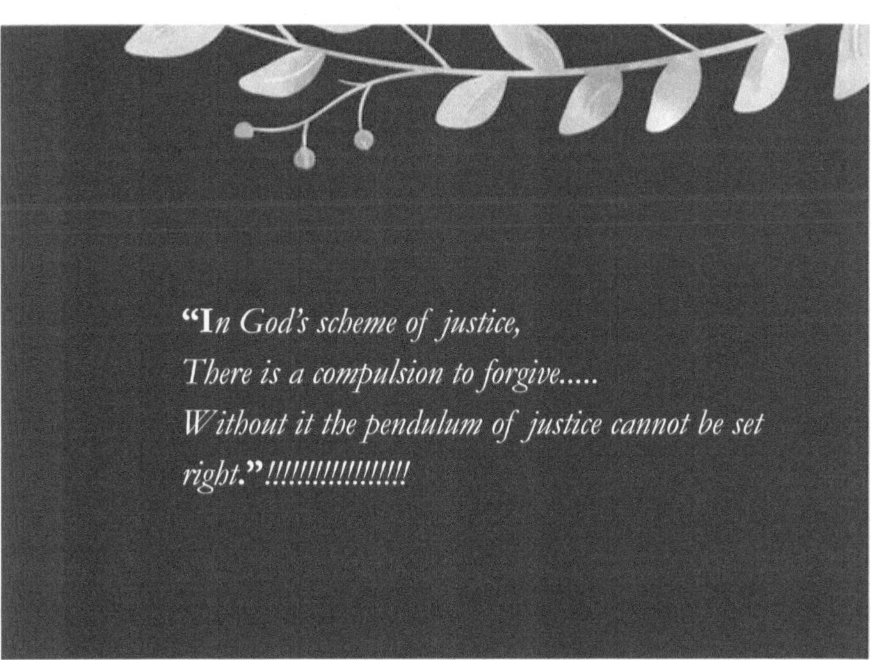
"In God's scheme of justice,
There is a compulsion to forgive.....
Without it the pendulum of justice cannot be set right."!!!!!!!!!!!!!!!!!

"In trusting God,
Reason is a bystander."!!!!!!!!!!!!!!!!!

"Imperfections are mandated by God...
Don't feel any guilt,
It's a way world is crafted."!!!!!!!!!!!!!!!!!!!!!

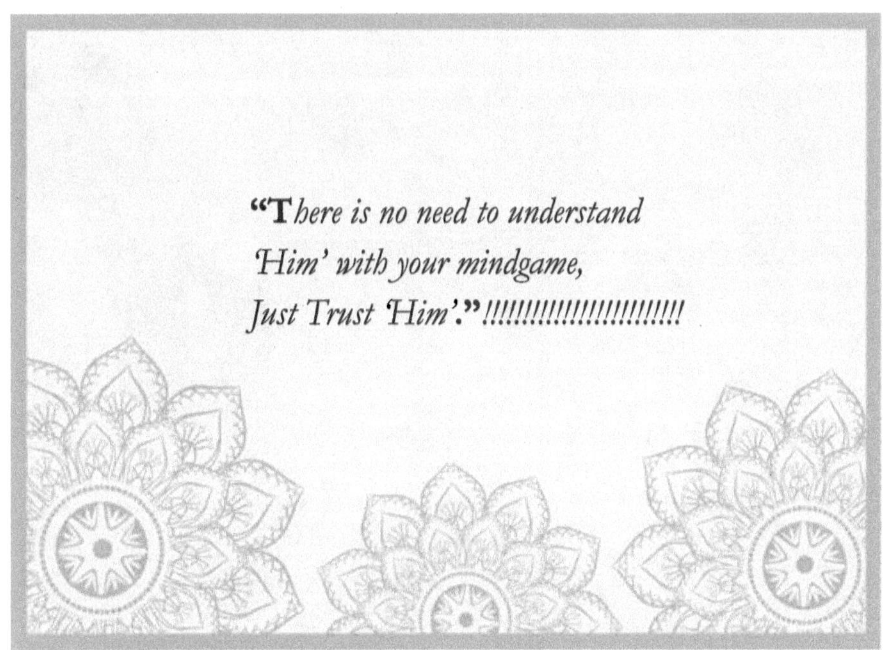
"There is no need to understand
'Him' with your mindgame,
Just Trust 'Him'."!!!!!!!!!!!!!!!!!!!!!!!!!

"Once you reach a certain age,
All that you want is just 'God'."!!!!!!!!!!!!!!!!!!!

"**W***e are dispatched by God,*
Only for a simple and compassionate living."!!!!!!!!!!!

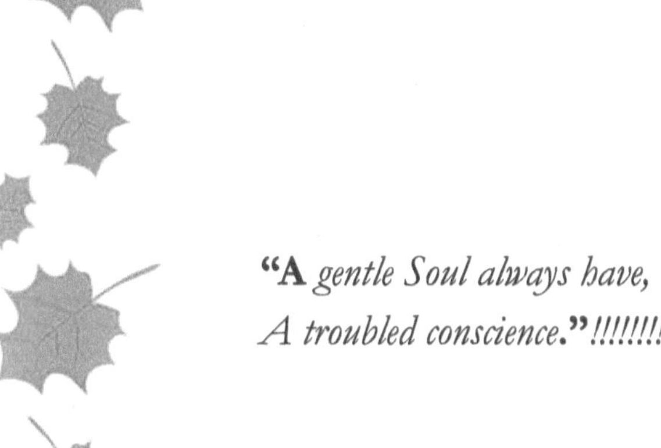

***"A** gentle Soul always have,*
A troubled conscience." !!!!!!!!!!!!!!!!!!!!!

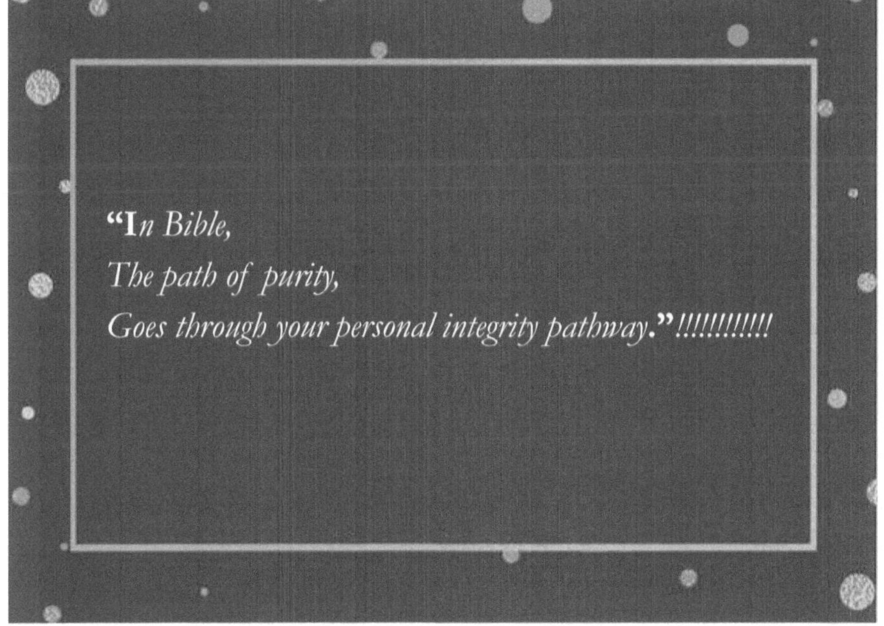

"Never be a man with empty meanings......
You never attain Salvation."!!!!!!!!!!!!!!!!!!!!!!!!!!!!!!!

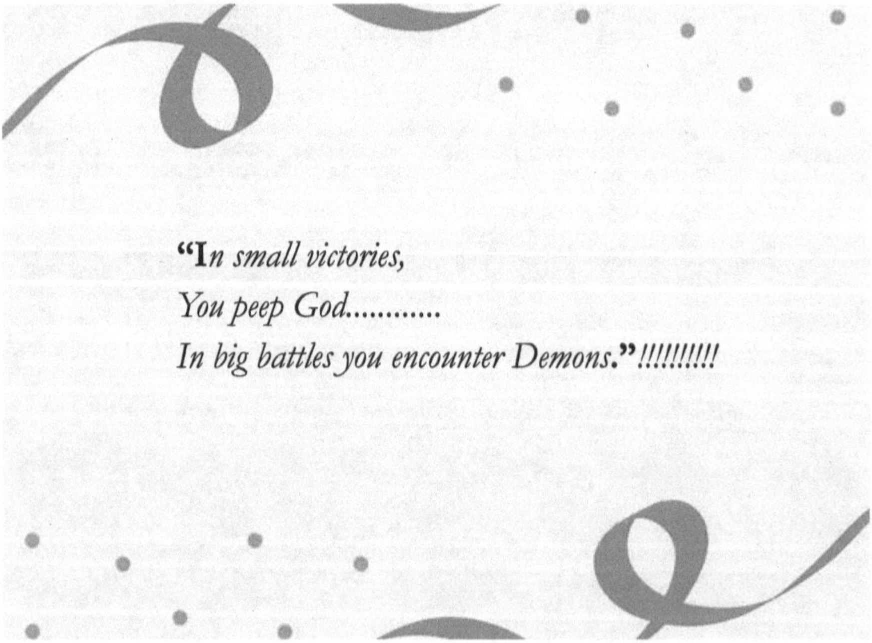

"In small victories,
You peep God............
In big battles you encounter Demons."!!!!!!!!!!

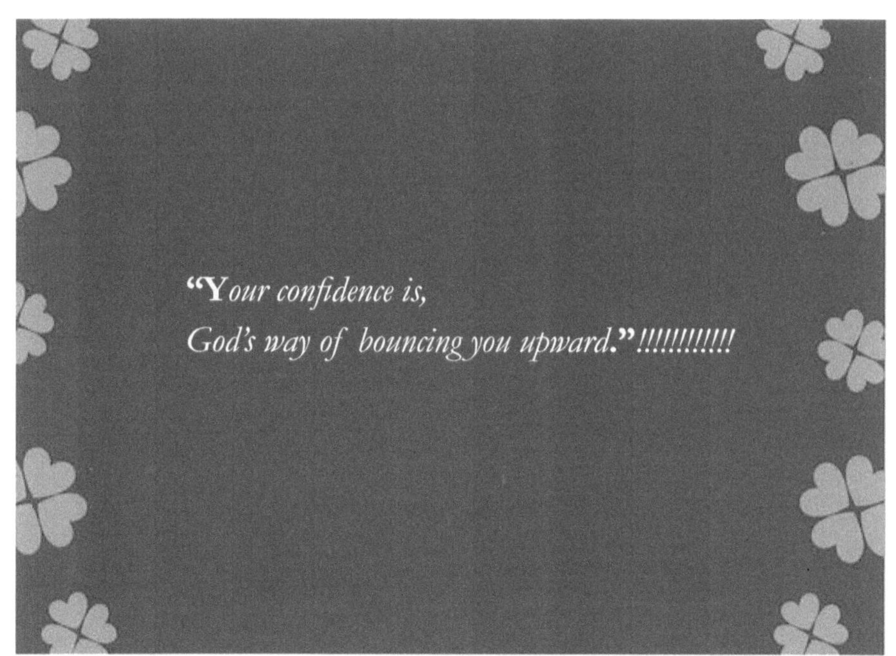

"Never rush into doing things, God has given you time.....................................
Never be made to rush into doing things, in both ways take your time, leisurely."!!!!!!!!!!!!!!!!!!!!

"**A** *Gratitudinal life,*
Reaches you,
Closer to God." *!!!!!!!!!!!!!!!!!!!!*

*"**W**ho is a Saint?*
A man who is above,
The craving to be appreciated."!!!!!!!!!!!!!!!!

*"**I** have lived madness for thirty years,*
God was there, and he gave back my sanity."!!!!!!!!!!!!!!!

Hope

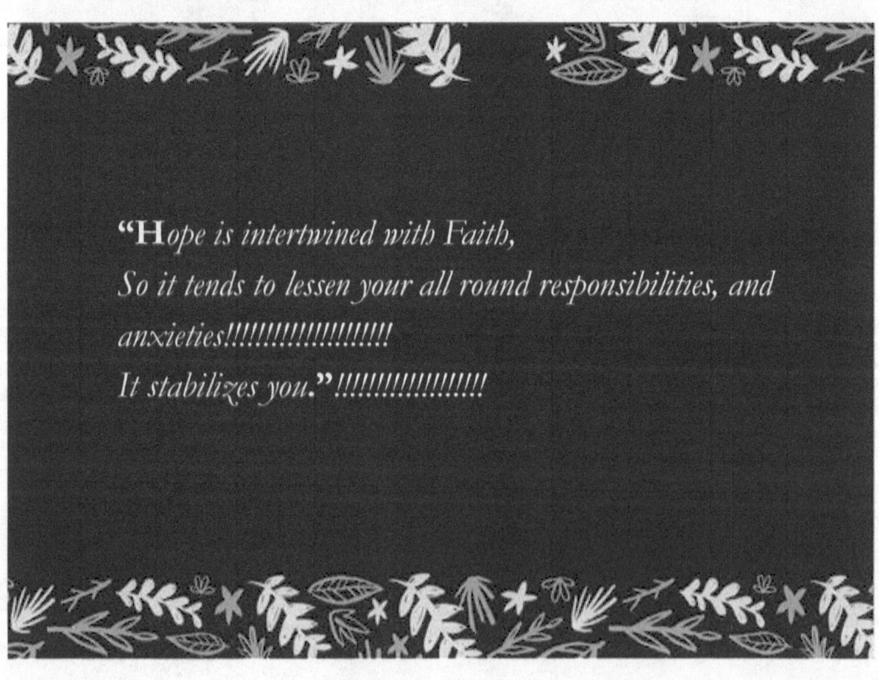
“Hope is intertwined with Faith,
So it tends to lessen your all round responsibilities, and anxieties!!!!!!!!!!!!!!!!!!!!!
It stabilizes you.” !!!!!!!!!!!!!!!!!!!

*"**I**f you trust your abilities*
Faith too gives a big push."!!!!!!!!!!!!!!!!!!!!

*"**F**aith kills fear*
It develops your persona."!!!!!!!!!!!!

*“ **F**aith’ is a Biblical forecast of the first order!!!!!!!!!!!!!!!!!!!!!!!*
If you have Faith, you would never sleep hungry.”!!!!!!!!!

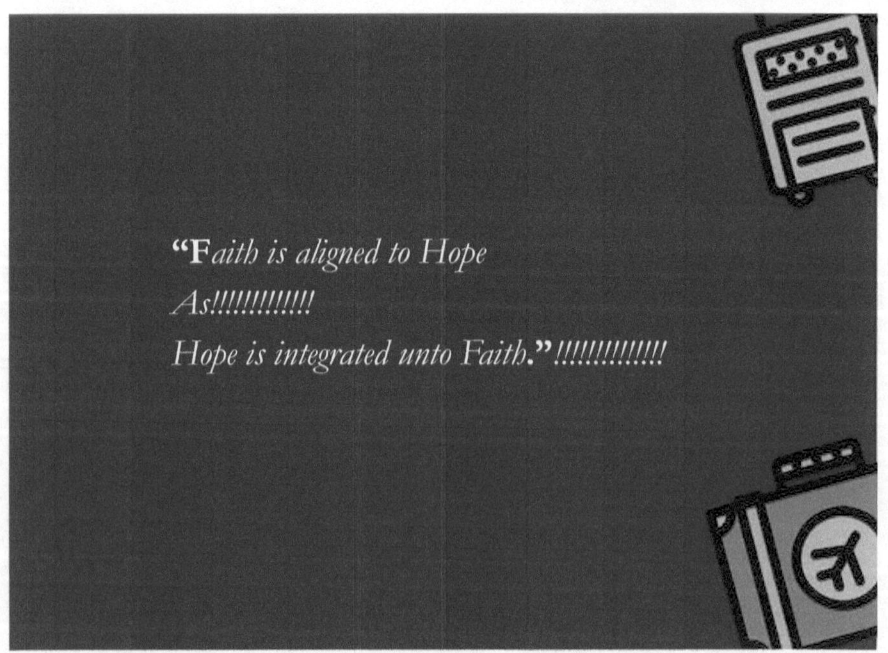

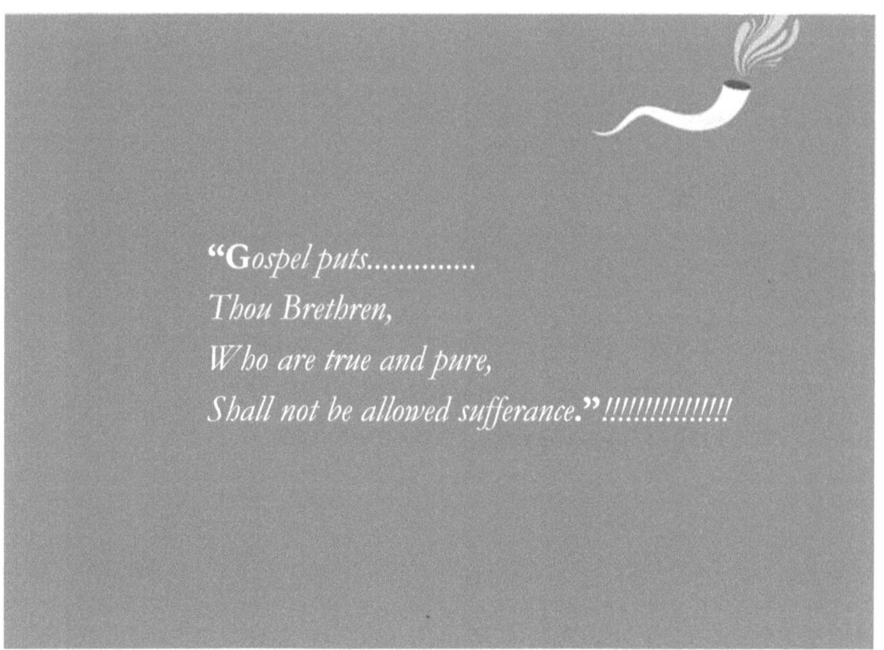

*"**G**ospel puts..............*
Thou Brethren,
Who are true and pure,
Shall not be allowed sufferance."!!!!!!!!!!!!!!!!

*"**I**f you fail,*
Take refuge unto Faith,
For it is a big ticket of your survival."!!!!!!!!!!!!!

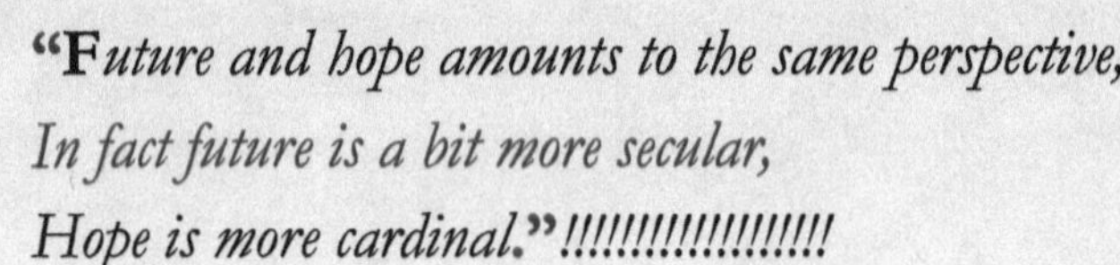

"**F***uture and hope amounts to the same perspective,*
In fact future is a bit more secular,
Hope is more cardinal."!!!!!!!!!!!!!!!!!!!!

"**M***ake Hope your ally,*
To face your life battles."!!!!!!!!!!!!!!!!!!!!

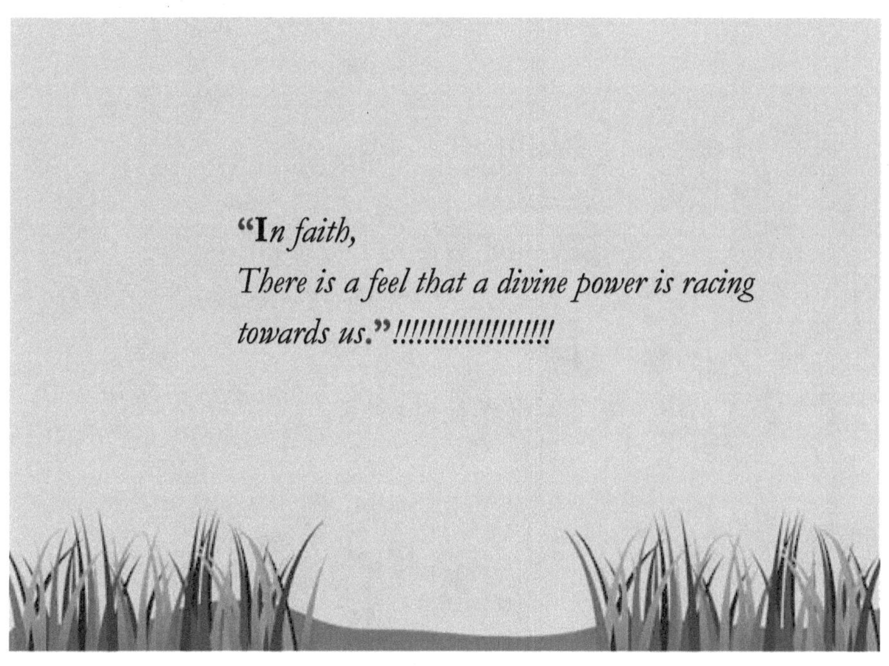

*"**H**ope knows no logic,*
It slays odds too..................
It has a mesmerising Fate." !!!!!!!!!!!!!!!!!!!!!!

"**H***ope is everyone's recipe,*
Though invisible,
It has endorsements in billion multiples,
It is spaceless and can be pocketed everywhere, all along
Brim with hope,
Believe in the goodness of things."!!!!!!!!!!!!!!!!!!!!!!!!!!!!!!

"**Y***our maturity is at its peak,*
Once you ordain Faithfulness."!!!!!!!!!!!!!

*"**O**nly from your heart,*
Can you touch your brethren."!!!!!!!!!!!

*"**H**ope is Blessed,*
It cannot be get lossed."!!!!!!!!!!!!!!!!!!!!!

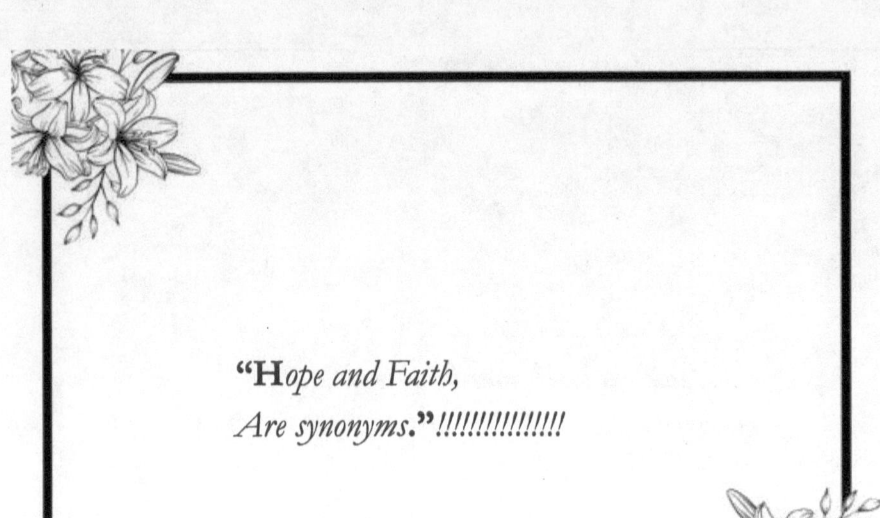
"**H***ope and Faith,*
Are synonyms." !!!!!!!!!!!!!!!!

"**H***ope fortifies Future,*
And gives it's meaning." !!!!!!!!!!!!!!!!

"Man is threadbare.......
He has only Hope."!!!!!!!!!!!!!!!!!!!!!!!!!

"The goalpost of fate
Can be empowered,
Only when you are hopeful."!!!!!!!!!!!!!!!!!!!!!

Leadership

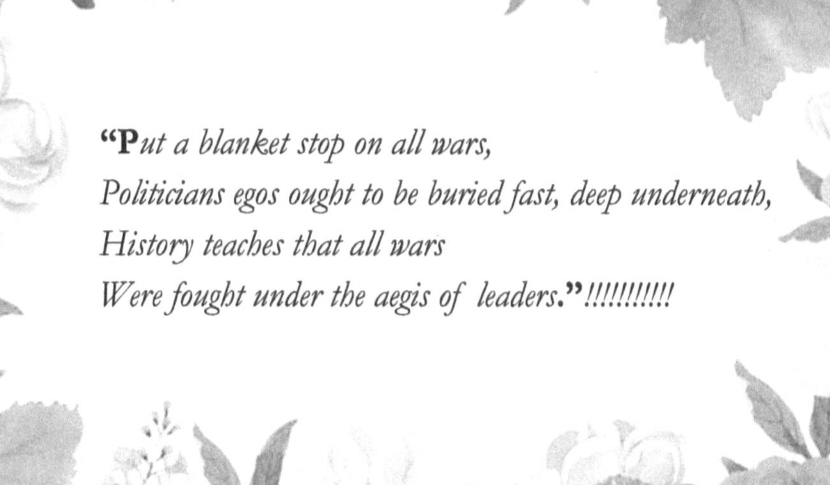

"**P***ut a blanket stop on all wars,*
Politicians egos ought to be buried fast, deep underneath,
History teaches that all wars
Were fought under the aegis of leaders."*!!!!!!!!!!!*

"**L***eaders are selfish,*
Tell me till date, if any leader has invested in people."*!!*

“L*eaders are not good in decision-making!!!!!!!!!*
The instinct to decide is getting weak as our Age progresses.” *!!!*

“I*n history,*
No leader has ever empowered others to lead.” *!!!!!!!!!!!!!!!*
!!!!!!!!!!!!!!!!!!!!

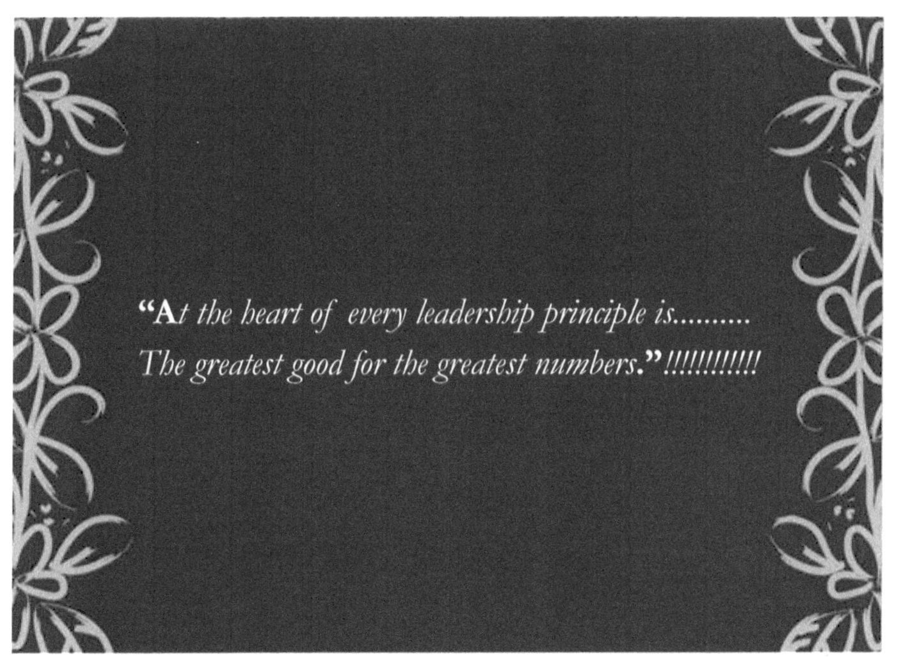
"At the heart of every leadership principle is..........
The greatest good for the greatest numbers." !!!!!!!!!!!!

"In these times,
Leadership has become a license,
for 'Doublespeak',
What leaders say, they never mean,
What they mean, they never say." !!!!!!!!!!!!

"**T***his Age leadership,*
Has failed to impact the coming generations,,,,,
Their ideals are misplaced." *!!!!!!!!!!!!!!!!!!!!!!!!!!*

"**A***ll across the spectrum..........*
Leadership has compromised itself,
For no pettier reason than clinging to
Power." *!!!!!!!!!!!!!!!*

"I*n the moment of crisis and danger, an intelligent Leadership!!!!!!!!!*
Either abdicates or
*Puts a cap on decision making.***"**!!!!!!!!!!!!!!!!!!!!!!!

"I*n this Age,*
We are cultivating a new breed of Leaders.........
*Leaders with zero followers.***"**!!!!!!!!!!!!!!!!!!!!!!!!

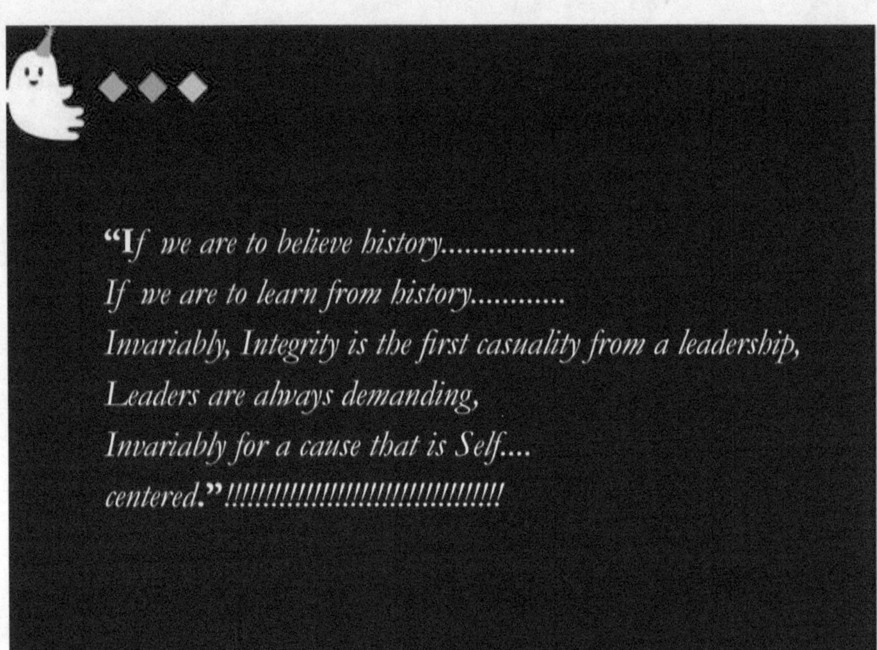
"If we are to believe history.................
If we are to learn from history............
Invariably, Integrity is the first casuality from a leadership,
Leaders are always demanding,
Invariably for a cause that is Self....
centered."!!!!!!!!!!!!!!!!!!!!!!!!!!!!!!!!!!!!!

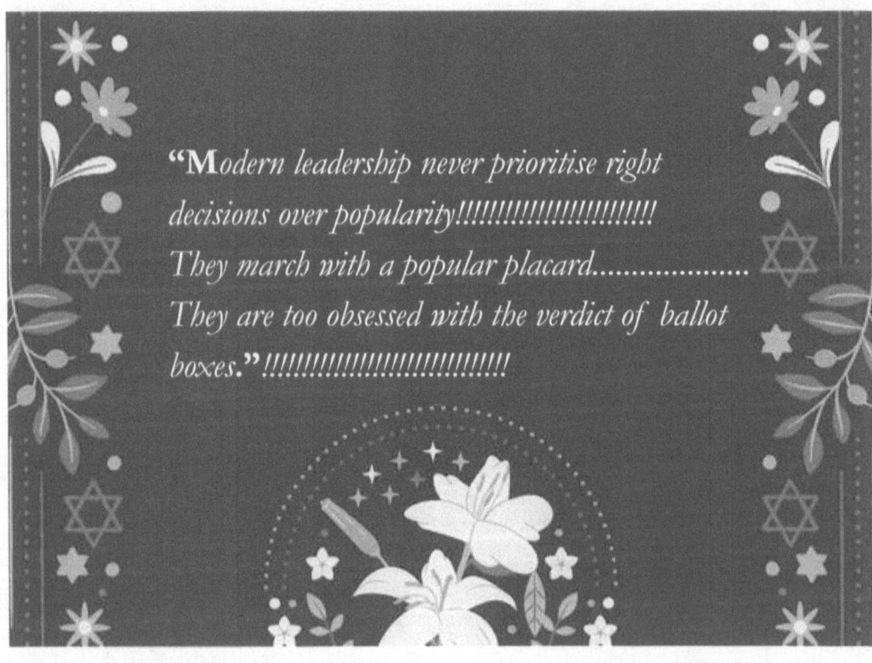
"Modern leadership never prioritise right
decisions over popularity!!!!!!!!!!!!!!!!!!!!!!!!!!!
They march with a popular placard...................
They are too obsessed with the verdict of ballot
boxes."!!!!!!!!!!!!!!!!!!!!!!!!!!!!!!!!!

"In the history of leaderships, since................
No leader has owned his share of blame,
And every leader has claimed his share of credit, fast."!!!!!!!!!!!!!!!!

"P*oliticians are worst listeners.*" *!!!!!!!!!!!!!!!!!!!!*

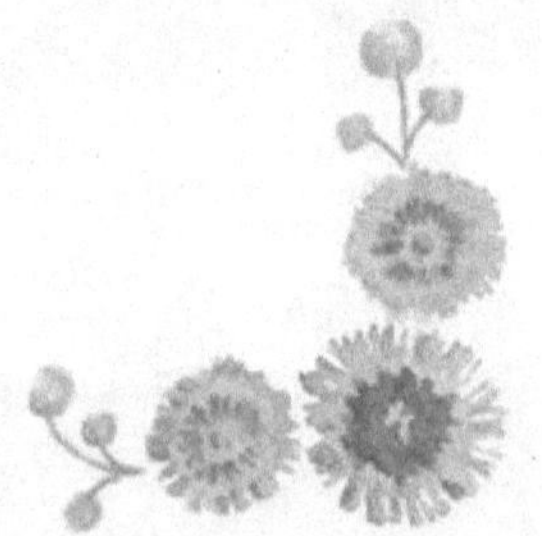

"H*umble leadership means,!!!!!!!!*
That a leader's concerns are genuine...........
That he stands for a commoner...........
That he leads from the grassroots." *!!!!!!!!!!!!!!*

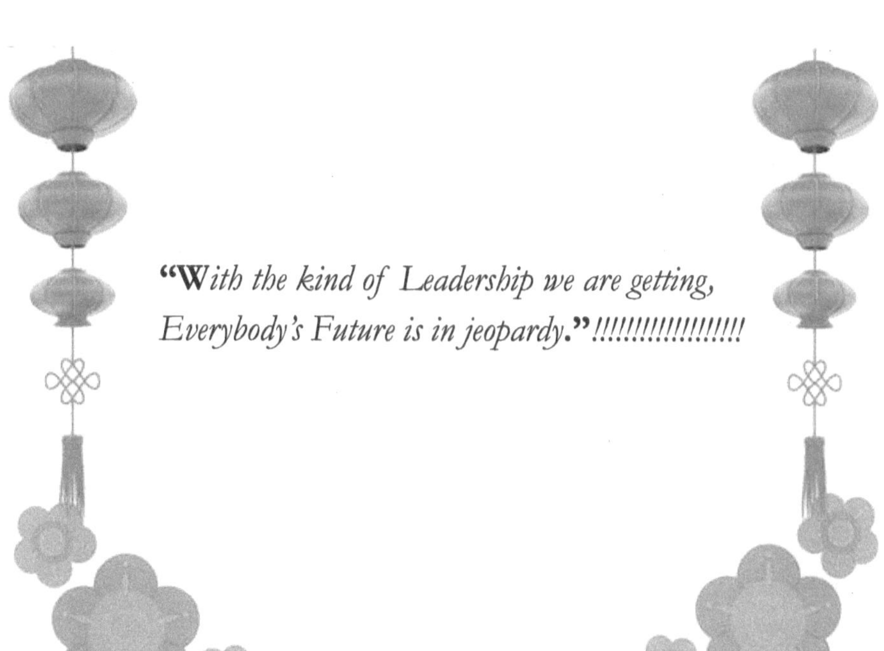

*“**W**ith the kind of Leadership we are getting,*
Everybody’s Future is in jeopardy.”!!!!!!!!!!!!!!!!!!!

*“**P**oliticians, Scientists, and Policy Makers,*
Are going for a great Reset,!!!!!!!!
For the growing aspirations of the wealthy.”!!!!!!!!!!!!!!!

"L*eaders are leading us to our graves............*
*They are sponsoring Wars.***"** !!!!!!!!!!!!!!!!!!!!!!!!!!!!!!!

"W*ar is a necessary evil,*
That we must endure.........
*History too began with wars.***"** !!!!!!!!!!!!!!!!!!

"**T***his Age Leadership,*
Is giving to people what they themselves are not having............,.
They are manifesting 'Assurances'." *!!!!!!!!!!!!!!!!!!*

"**D***ecision-Making is one area where AI cannot compete with Human -ingenuity!!!!!!!!*
Machines cannot make man a mere spectator!!!!!!!!!
He is a necessary evil,
Since." *!!!!!!!!!!!!!!!!!!!!!!!!!!!!!!*

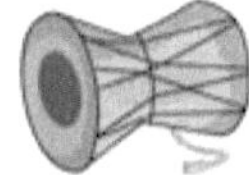

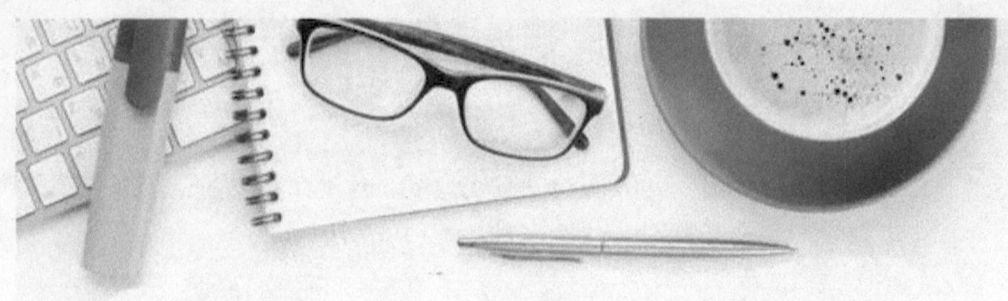

*“**L**eadership is predominantly a male domain,*
Never inject females here,,,,,,,,,,,
For then you would suffer an ineffective governance.” !!!!!!!!!!!!!!!!!!!!

Family

"S*ufferance at the hands of our near and dear ones,*
Is the redeeming life-lesson that we learn in going
through life."!!!!!!!!!!!!!!!!!!!!!!!!!!!

"W*hat our children need most,*
Is that they become fearless............,
It makes them strong and confident."!!!!!!!!!!!!!!!!!!!!

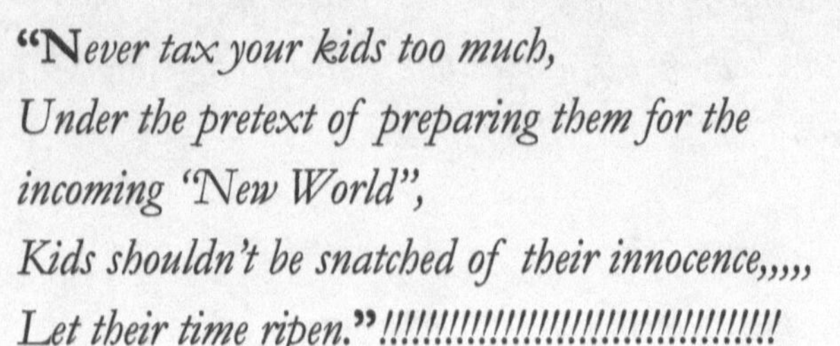

"**N***ever tax your kids too much,*
Under the pretext of preparing them for the incoming "New World",
Kids shouldn't be snatched of their innocence,,,,,
Let their time ripen." !!

"**T***hose who help and guide, are the first to be forgotten,*
This is how, the law of upbringing wor ks." !!

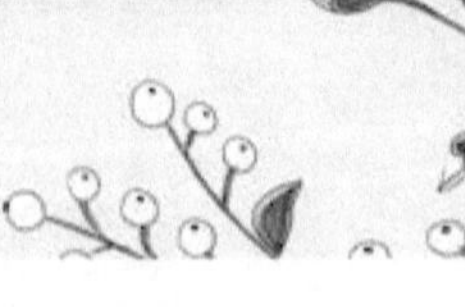

"I'*m jealous of my Parents...........*
I'll never have a kid as cool as theirs."!!!!!!!!!!!!!!!

"A *real and honest man is priceless for a women,*
A caring and value driven women is platinum,
Be judicious in your choices for a mate."!!!!!!!!!!!!!!!!!!!!

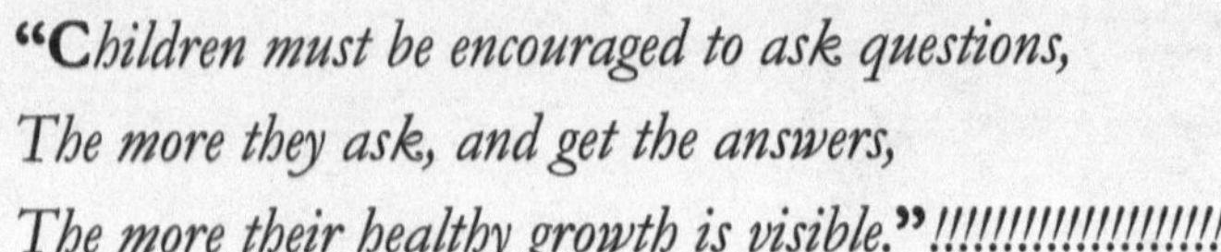

"Children must be encouraged to ask questions,
The more they ask, and get the answers,
The more their healthy growth is visible."!!!!!!!!!!!!!!!!!!!!

"Always make yourself,
Your first love,!!!!!!!!!!
Your parents must be placed then, and
Thereafter must come, the love for your beloved,
Never disturb the given order."!!!!!!!!!!!!!!!!!!!!!!!!!!!!!

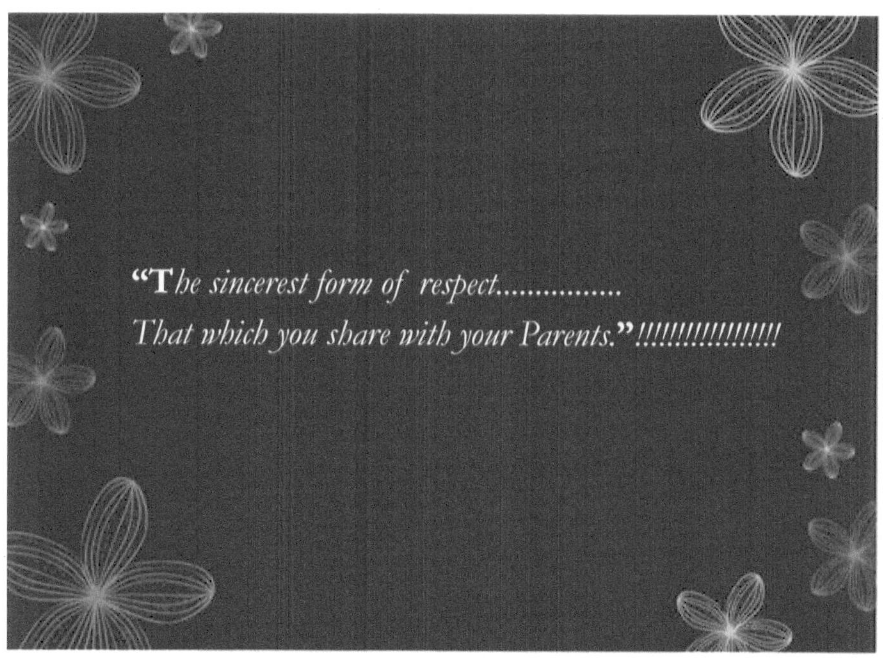

"The sincerest form of respect................
That which you share with your Parents."!!!!!!!!!!!!!!!!!!

"Be there for your Parents,
Be there for your neighbours too."!!!!!!!!!!!!!!!!!!!!!!!

"*You are what your parents and*
grandparents!!!!!!!
Wished for, prayed for and sacrificed for.........
Pray for them, and never be in a habit of
disobeying them." !!!!!!!!!!!!!!!!!!!!!!!!!!!!!!!

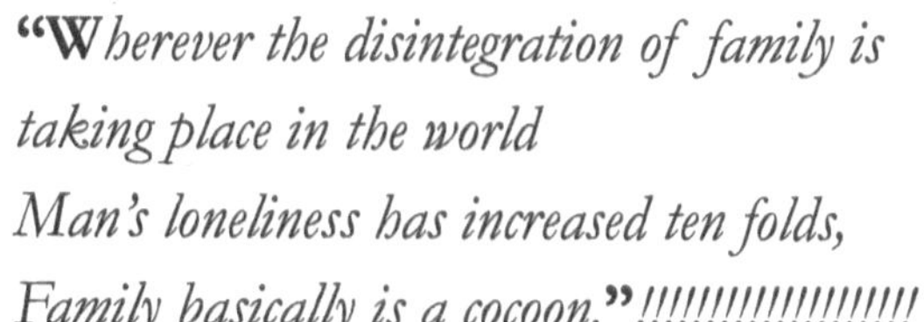
"Wherever the disintegration of family is
taking place in the world
Man's loneliness has increased ten folds,
Family basically is a cocoon."!!!!!!!!!!!!!!!!!!!!

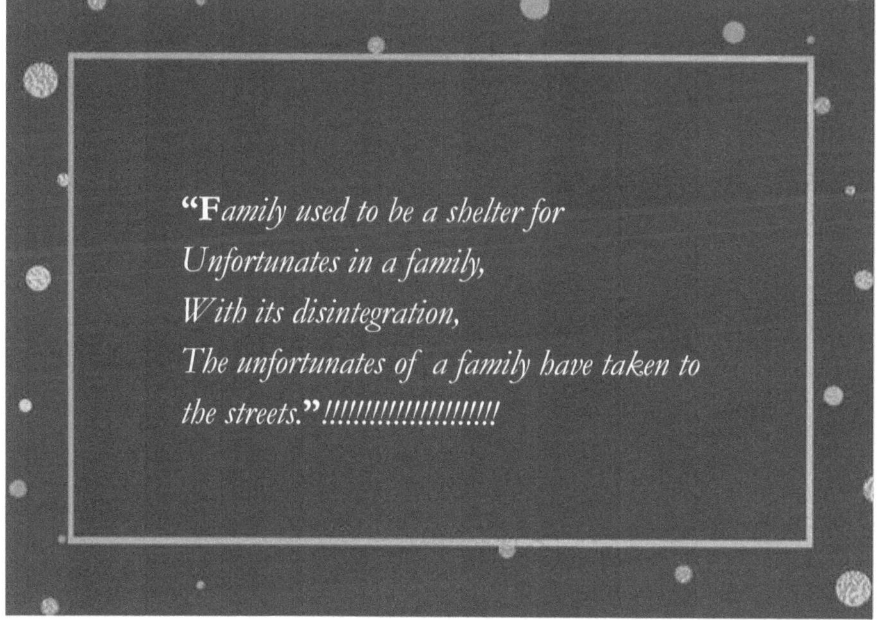
"Family used to be a shelter for
Unfortunates in a family,
With its disintegration,
The unfortunates of a family have taken to
the streets."!!!!!!!!!!!!!!!!!!!!!!

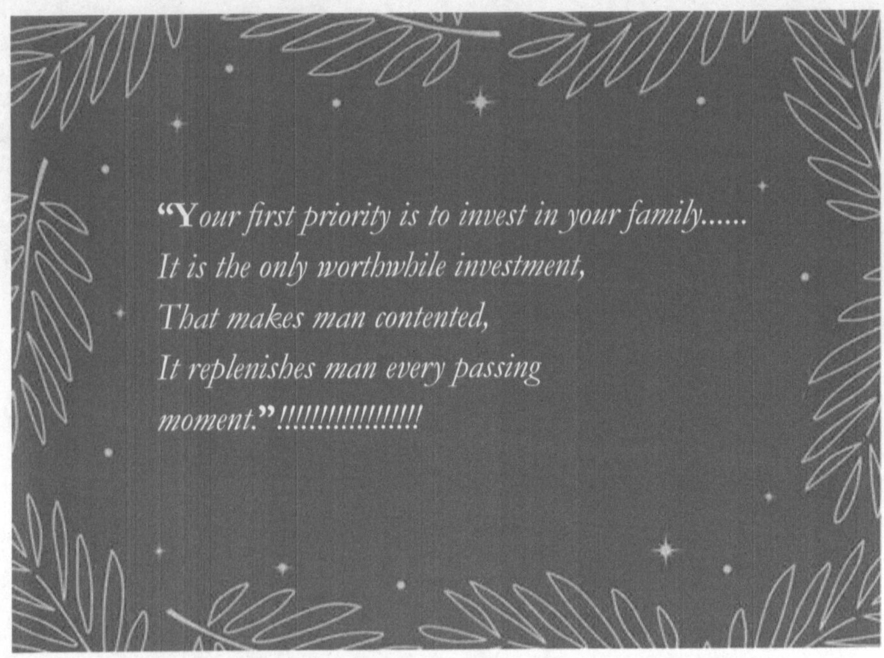

*"When you count your Blessings,
Give the benefit of doubt to your
Family!!!!!!
Count it Twice."!!!!!!!!!!!!!!!!!!!!!!!!!!!*

"**A** *family is a rock........*
Which is embedded in selflessness." !!!!!!!!!!!!!!!

"**P***arents deserve forgiveness.*" !!!!!!!!!!!!!!!!!!!!

*"**R**ich parents never,*
Can procreate caring, sensible and non-attitudinal siblings."!!!!!!!!!!!!!!!!!!

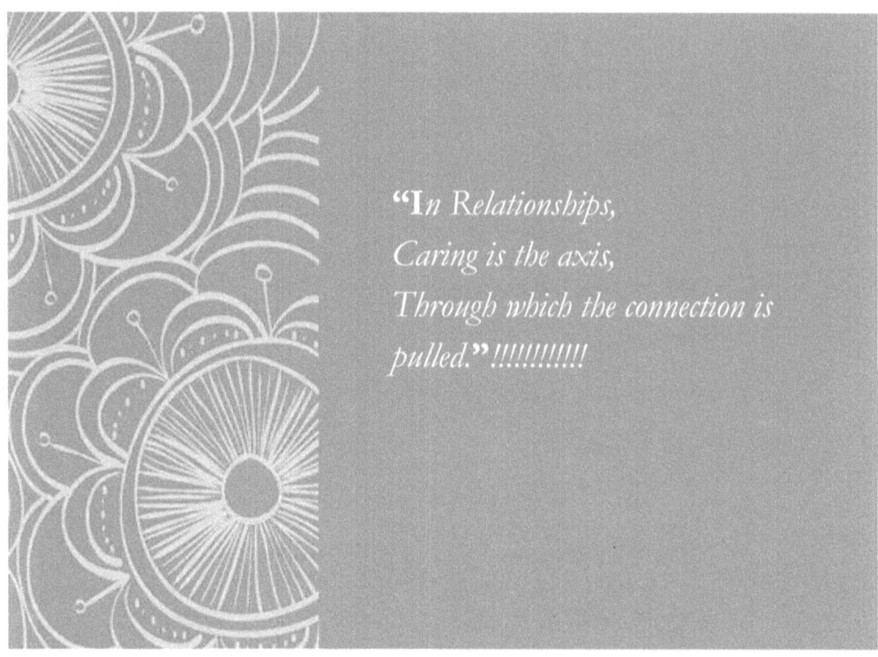
"In Relationships,
Caring is the axis,
Through which the connection is
pulled." !!!!!!!!!!!

"Who will die first,
Husband or wife ....
Makes the fate deep." !!!!!!!!!!!!!!!!!!!!!!

*"**S**upport and help rarely comes from near and dear ones..............*
An acquaintance is always more supportive." !!!!!!!!!!!!!

*"**B**ecoming a parent,*
is a life time bliss." !!!!!!!!!!!!!

"**A** *father imparts fearlessness in his siblings..............*
While a mother imparts the virtues of patience."*!!!!!!!!!!!!!!!!*

"**I***n these times,*
Rich parents are not proving a blessing for their siblings,
They neither have time,
Nor they have attitude for a healthy upbringing."*!!!!!!!!!!!!!!!!!!*

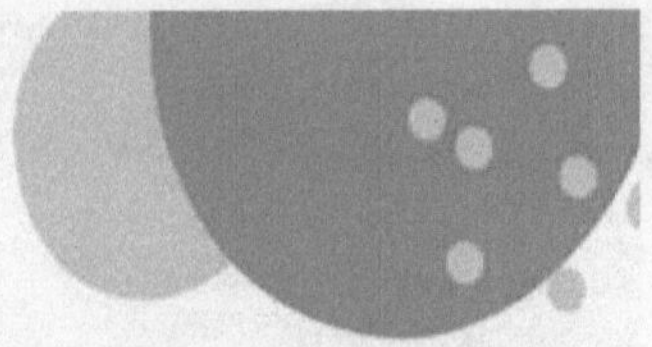

*"**A**lways help your child to understand life..........*
And make preparation for him to face it.........
Inculcate him to a simplify living." !!!!!!!!!!!!!!!!!!!!!!

*"**N**ever rush into a marriage,*
Take your time,
You will not regret." !!!!!!!!!!!!!!!!!!!!!!

"T*he growth and learning of a kid,*
Is socially more permeating and interesting,
*Than that of a grown up man's learning.***"** *!!!!!!!!!!!!!!!!!!*

"A *family no longer remains a place,*
Where members are interested in simply bringing
*out the best in each of us.***"** *!!!!!!!!!!!!!!!!!!!!!!!!!!!*

"**I***n our relationship arena,*
Some people are never allowed to speak up their mind,
For their remaining dumb, suits everybody."!!!!!!!!!!!!!!!

"**I***t is a riddle?*
A mother is always jealous of her grown up daughter..............
On the contrary, a father is always proud of his grown up son."!!!!!!!!!!!!!!!!!!!!!!!

"G*ive quality time to your child,*
*It nourishes a child's self-esteem.***"** !!!!!!!!!!!!!!!!!

"N*ever decide a career for your child,*
*Ask him to choose one.***"** !!!!!!!!!!!!!!!!!!!!!

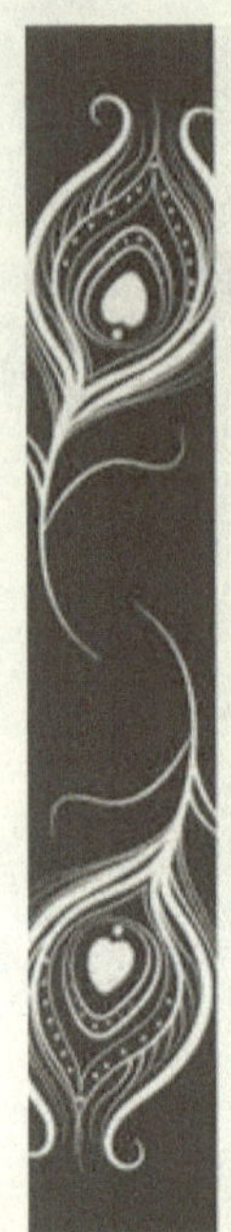

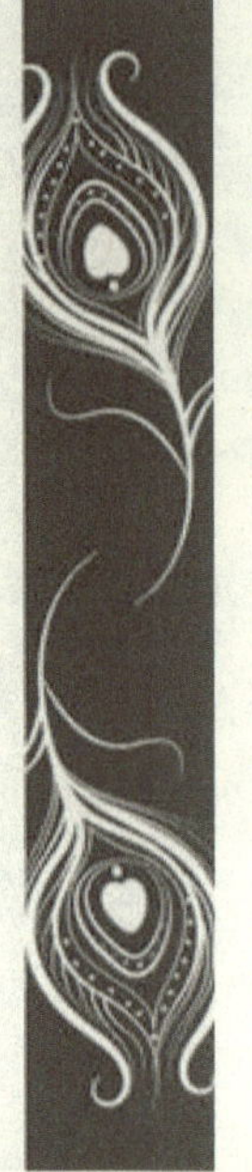

*"**L**oving a son, for a mother, is always more gratifying,*
Than loving her daughter."!!!!!!!!!!!!!!!!!!!

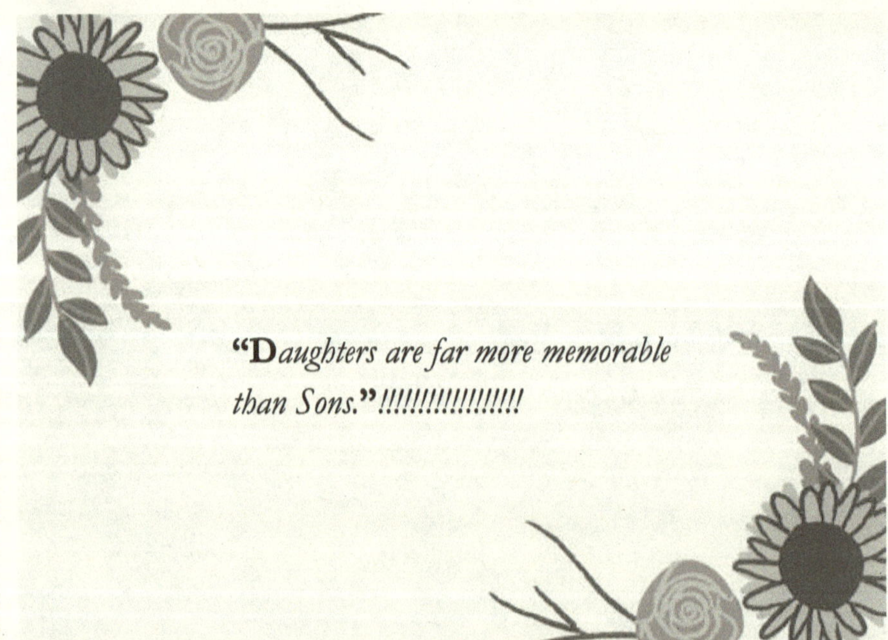

*"**D**aughters are far more memorable than Sons."*!!!!!!!!!!!!!!!!!!

Society

"People rarely respect themselves,
They delegate this act to others,
And seek validation from others!!!!!!!!!!!!!!!!!!!
This is putting the cart before the bullock."!!!!!!!!

"**M***istakes are value driven.*"!!!!!!!!!!!!!!!!!!!!!!!!!!!!!!

"**Y***our failings and your fall*
Are situations that are bound to occur, and reoccur too often,
Your maturity lies in presenting a" Brave" front,
Every man is made to suffer odd situations."!!!!!!!!!!!!!!!!!

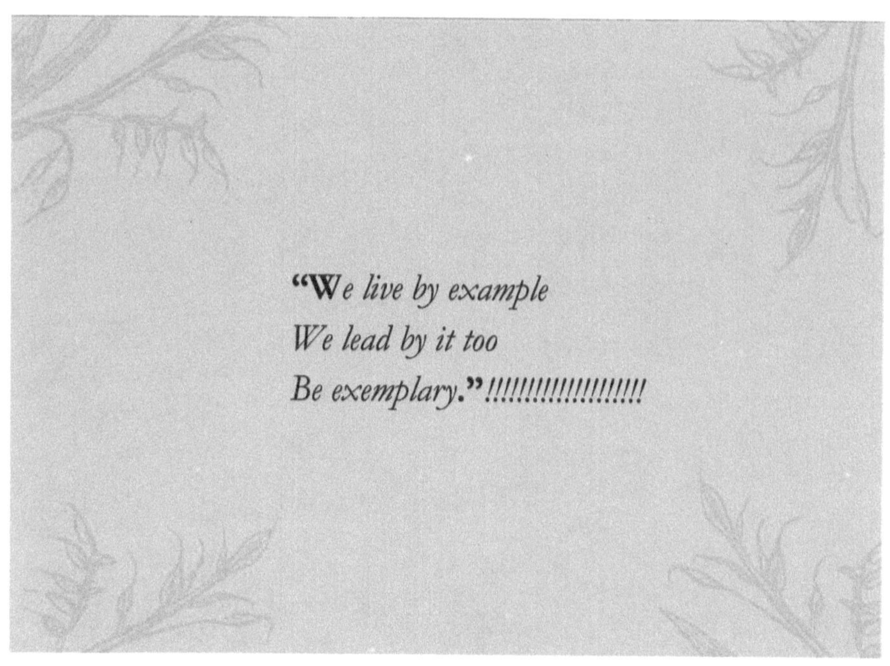

"S*elfish people are neither capable of loving others,*
Nor they are capable of loving themselves,,,,,,,,,,,
Just so, they live in a state of mental flux."!!!!!!!!!!!!!!!!!!!!

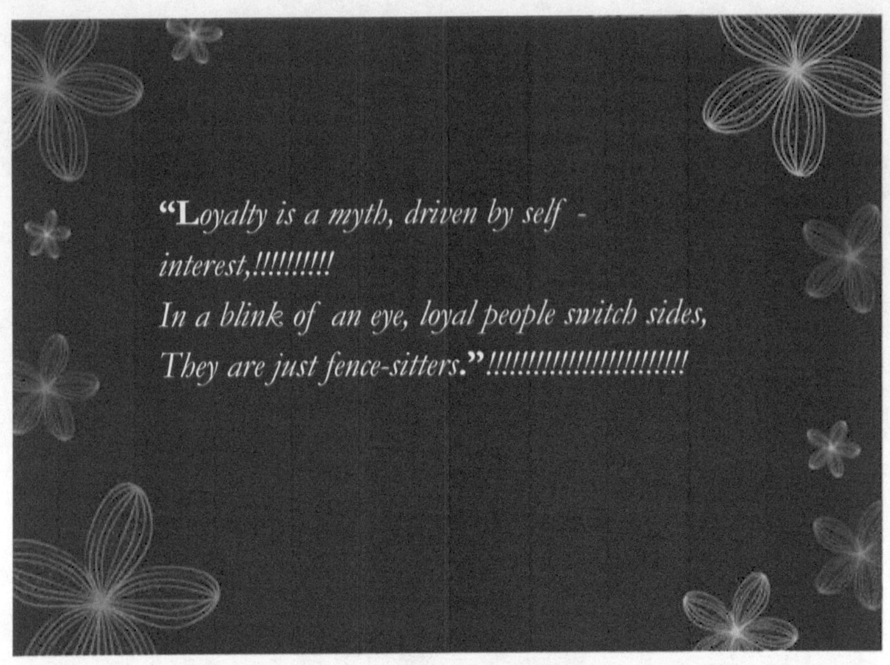
"Loyalty is a myth, driven by self - interest,!!!!!!!!!!
In a blink of an eye, loyal people switch sides,
They are just fence-sitters."!!!!!!!!!!!!!!!!!!!!!!!!!!!!

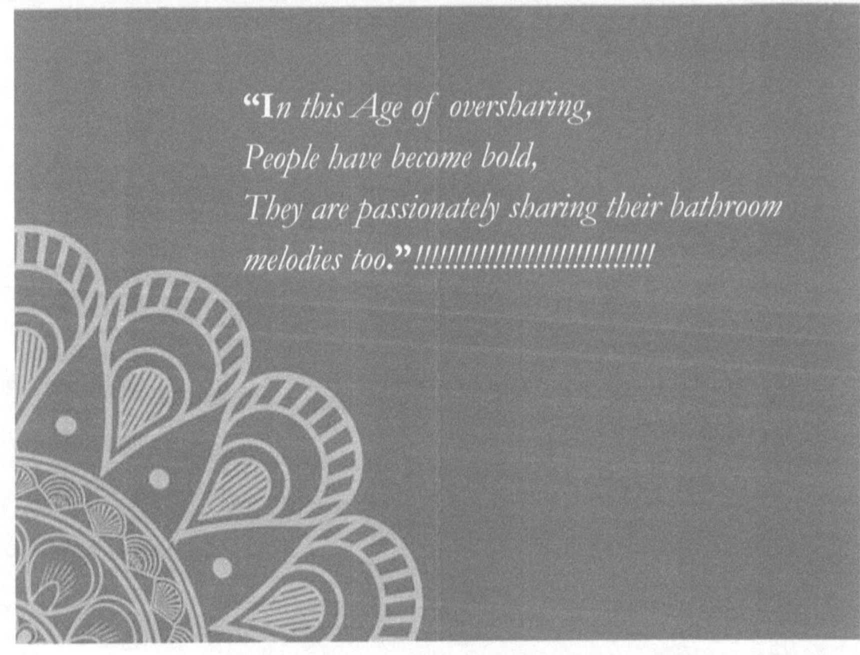
"In this Age of oversharing,
People have become bold,
They are passionately sharing their bathroom melodies too."!!!!!!!!!!!!!!!!!!!!!!!!!!!!!!!!

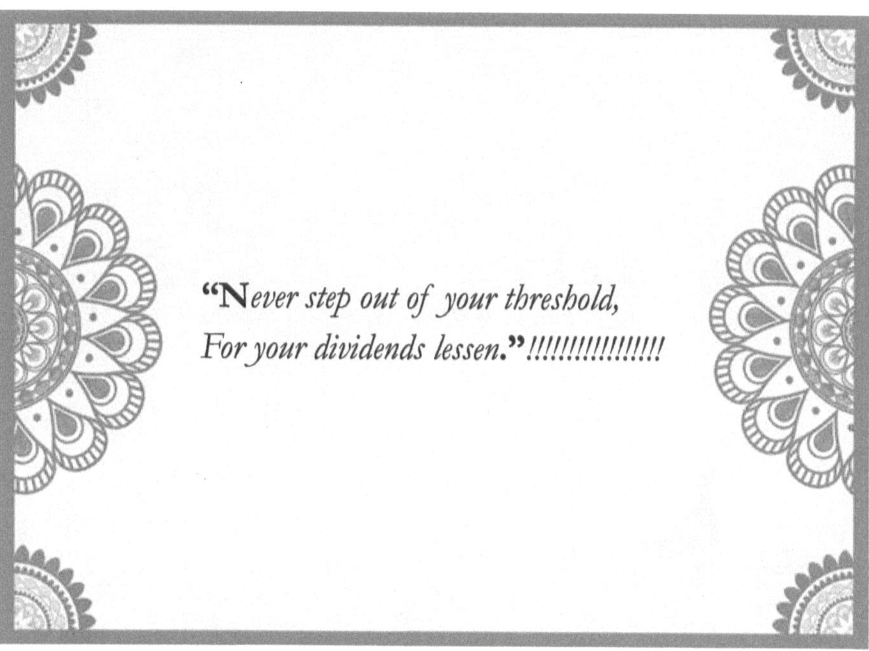

"In life your awareness is supreme..............
It ticks perpetually through your soul,,,,,,,,,,,,,,,
While Beliefs are secondary and sectarian,
they aren't foundational."
!!!!!!!!!!!!!!!!!!!!!!!!!!!!!!!

"**A***nger, fear, ego jealousy,*
Together or even one at a time, anniliates a man."!!!!!!!!!!!!

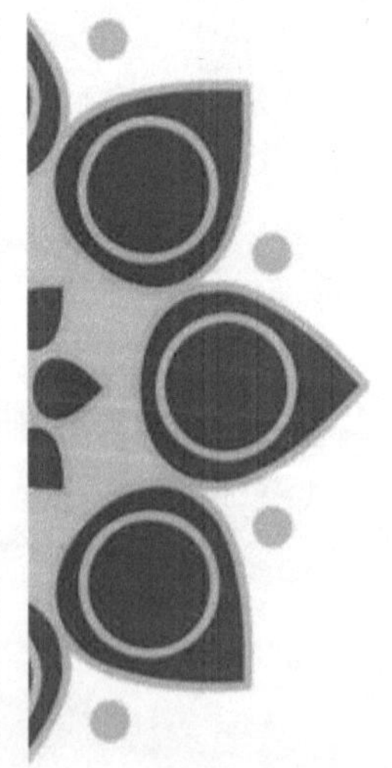

"**I***n sadness, what people expect,*
Is sharing their grief,!!!!!!!!!!!!!!!
A grief shared, is a grief lessened."!!!!!!!!!!!!!!!!

*"**I**n a society,*
Its inclusivity is the Elixir." !!!!!!!!!!!!!!!!!!!!

*"**N**ever give cash to a beggar,*
Always give him food for his hunger,
You should know that beggary is a multibillion dollar industry,
It is being oiled by fakeness." !!!!!!!!!!!!!!!!!!!!!!!!!!!

*"**F**ools can never be convinced of their foolishness..........*
They always take pride in themselves,
Their sense of right and wrong is mistakenly poised." !!!!!!!!!!!!!!!!!

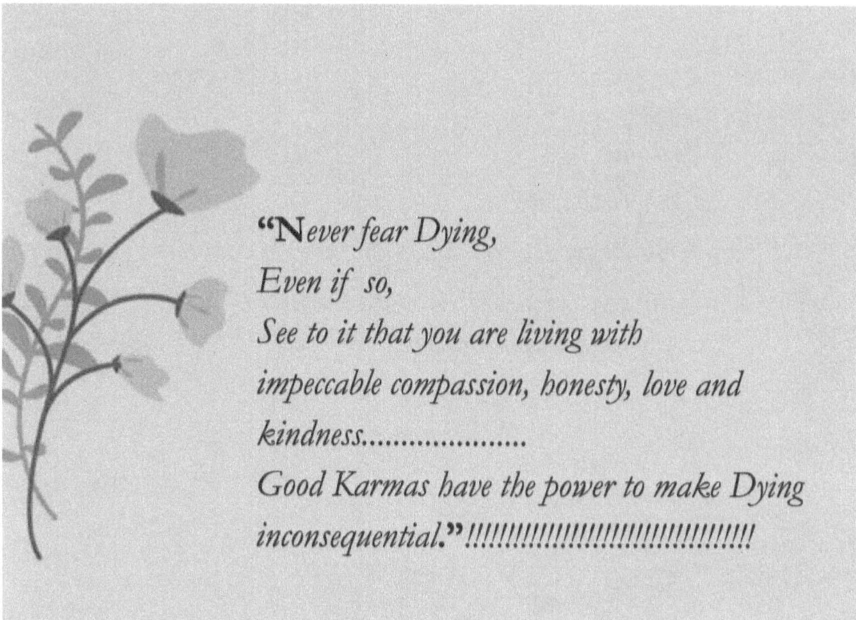
“Never fear Dying,
Even if so,
See to it that you are living with
impeccable compassion, honesty, love and
kindness....................
Good Karmas have the power to make Dying
inconsequential.”!!

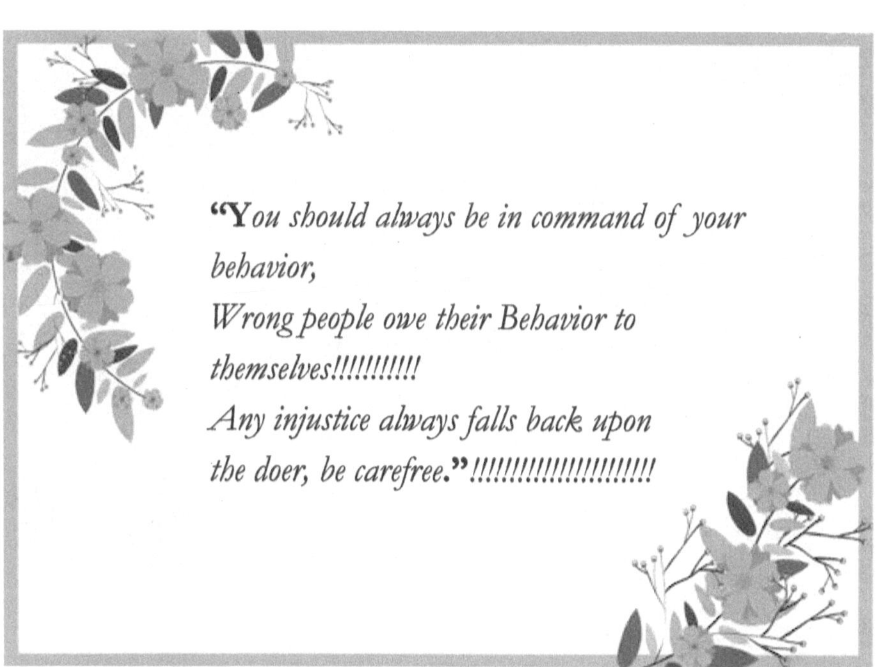
“You should always be in command of your
behavior,
Wrong people owe their Behavior to
themselves!!!!!!!!!!!
Any injustice always falls back upon
the doer, be carefree.”!!!!!!!!!!!!!!!!!!!!!!!!

"**I***n our Age,*
Love victimizes...........
It no longer has remained pristine...........
Your near and dear ones are the first to drain you." *!!!!!!!!!!!!!!!!!!!!!!!!!!!!*

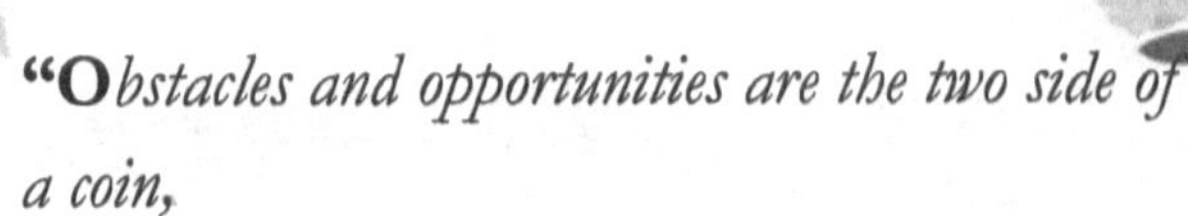

"**O***bstacles and opportunities are the two side of a coin,*
In obstacles there are seeds of opportunity,
In opportunity there are seeds of growth." *!!!!!!!!!!!!!!!!!!*

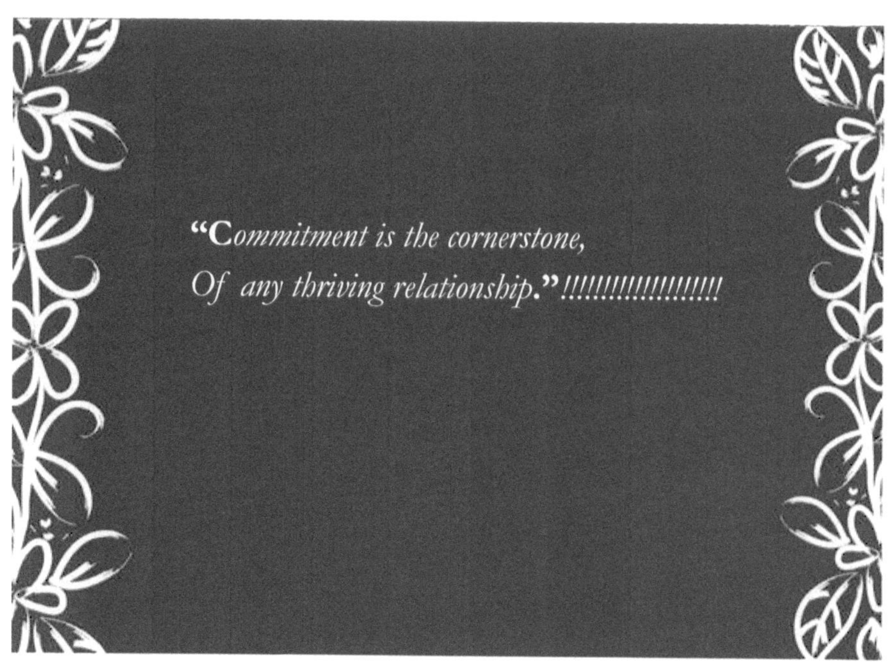

"Jealousies always comes from near and dear,,
You are helpless,
You can't do much."!!!!!!!!!!!!!!!!!!!!!!!!!!!!!!!!!!

"In relationships,
You have to give more,
And receive less,,,,,,,,,,,,
Then things will work better."!!!!!!!!!!!!!!!!!!!!!!!!!!

"It is seen across the spectrum,
Those you help, with time become your adversaries,
Moreover, with time you become inconsequential for them."!!!!!!!!!!!!!!!!!!!!!!!!!

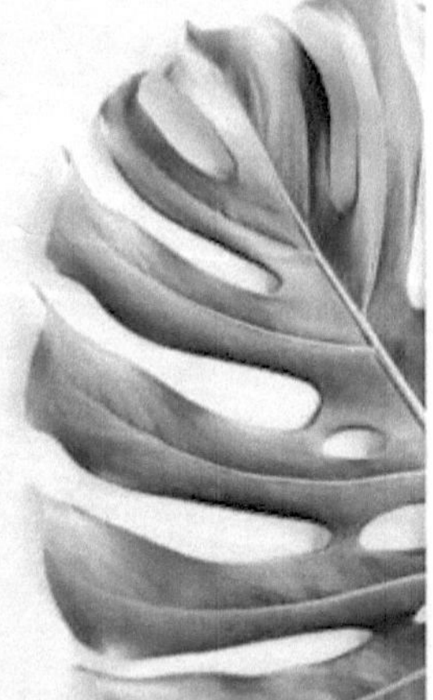

*"**T**he infirmity of a free mind is,*
That it becomes too self-centered,
A free mind rather turns an anarchist,
as History says."!!

*"**T**oday Man is facing too much alienation,,,,,,,,,,,,*
And this is prominently seen in his increasing love for animals and pets."!!!!!!!!!!!!!!!!!!!!!!!!!!!

*"**B**usiness thrives when,*
There is a division of Responsibility,
More so,
Also of Accountability." !!!!!!!!!!!!!!!!!!!!!!

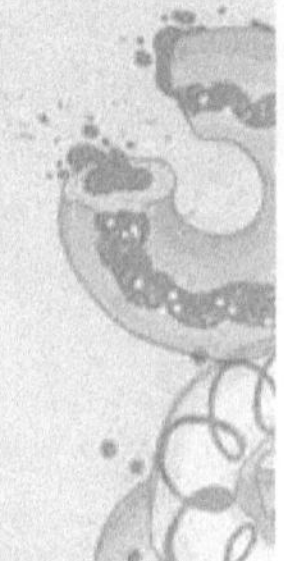

*"**S**trength of community has a*
unmatched profundity!!!!
Nurture communities,
Otherwise we all become
aliens." !!!!!!!!!!!!!!!!!!!!!!!!!!!!!!!

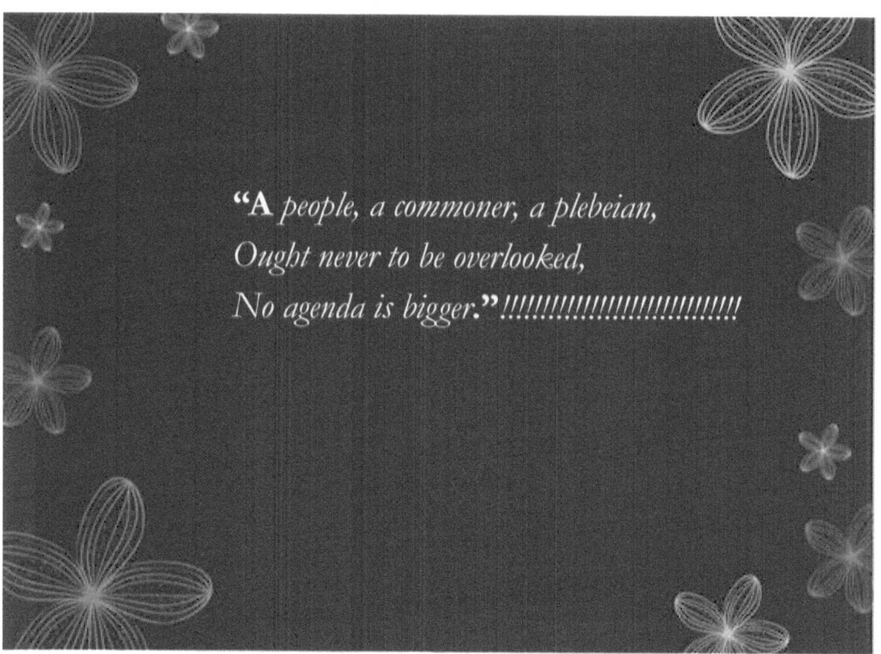

"There is a dearth of good decision
makers in this Age!!!!!!!!!!!
Why so?
Just because people are
scared to take and owe
responsibility."!!

"Give more,
receive less in life!!!!!!!!!!!!!
For better social enrichment."!!!!!!!!!!!!!

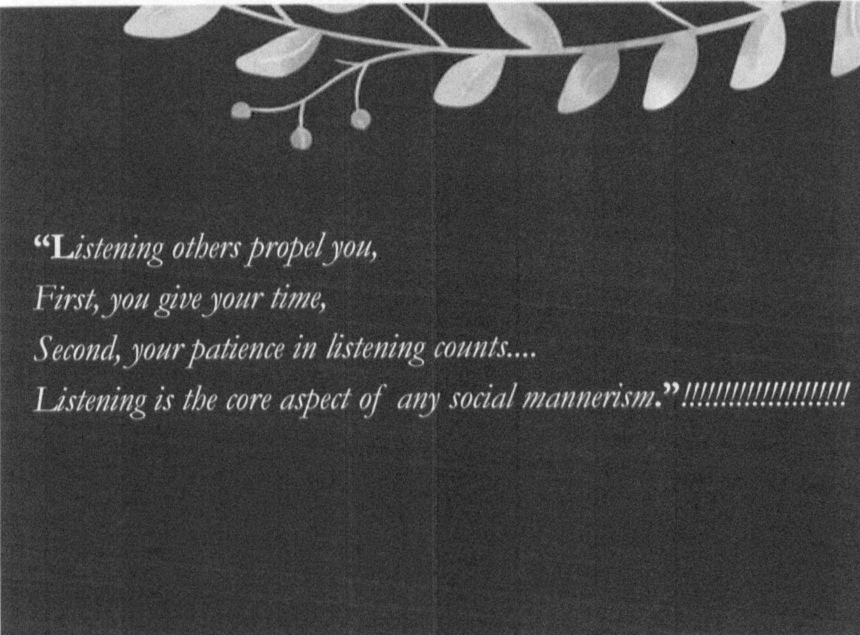
"Listening others propel you,
First, you give your time,
Second, your patience in listening counts....
Listening is the core aspect of any social mannerism."!!!!!!!!!!!!!!!!!!!!

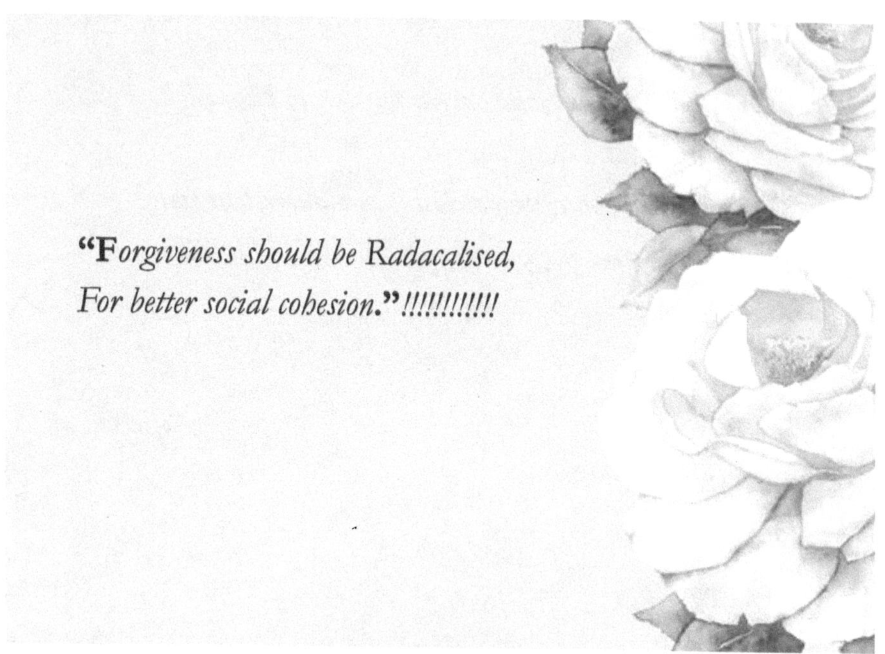
"Forgiveness should be Radacalised,
For better social cohesion."!!!!!!!!!!!!

"Inclusion gives our social fabric,
A rhythmic poise."!!!!!!!!!!!!!!!!!!!!

"Today everyone have a passion to built high walls.................
Maybe today we are losing our interest in even seeing our neighbours face." !!!!!!!!!!!!!!!!!!!!!!!!!

"O*ne should learn the art of self rewarding,*
You can pat on your back for your healthy choices and habits!!!!!!!!!!
Recent researches of neurosciences say that this increases
Your dopamine levels,
You become robust and healthy." !!!!!!!!!!!!!!!!!!!!

"W*e should learn to grow together*
And accompany people of all shades in our Journey,
Towards a destination which fulfills
Everyone's dream." !!!!!!!!!!!!!!!!!!!!!!!!!!!!!

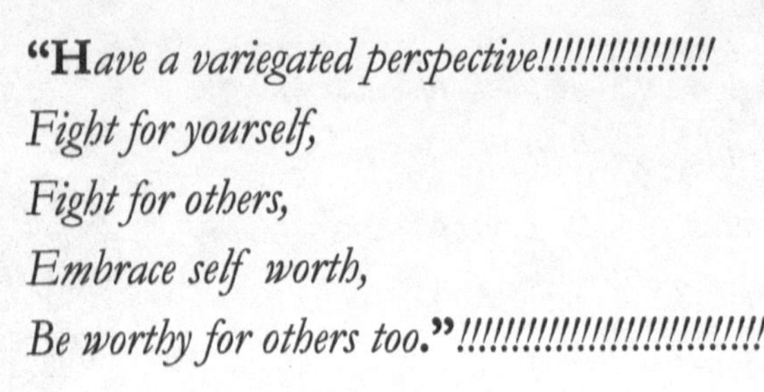
“**H***ave a variegated perspective!!!!!!!!!!!!!!!!*
Fight for yourself,
Fight for others,
Embrace self worth,
Be worthy for others too.” *!!!!!!!!!!!!!!!!!!!!!!!!!!!!!!*

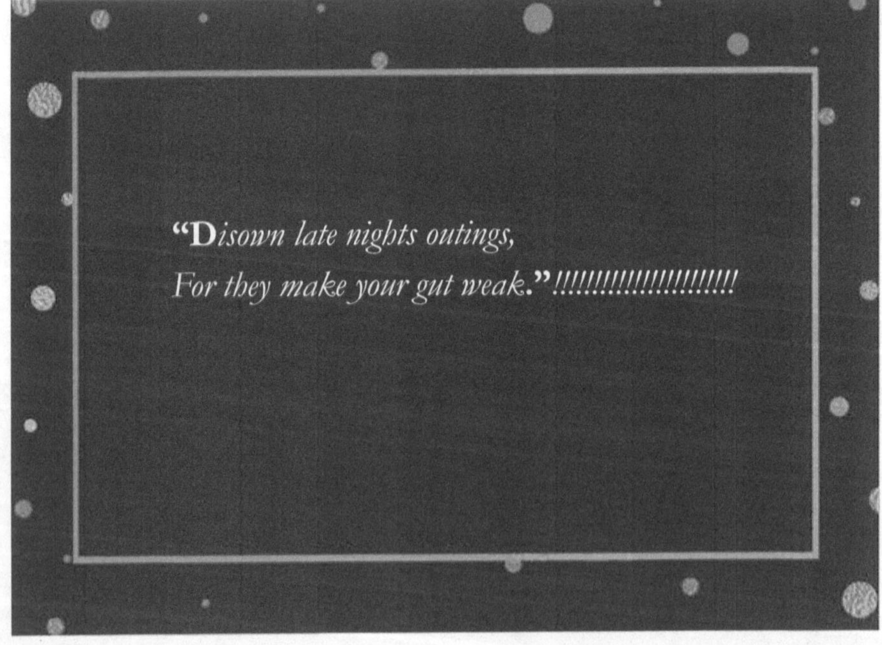
“**D***isown late nights outings,*
For they make your gut weak.” *!!!!!!!!!!!!!!!!!!!!!!!*

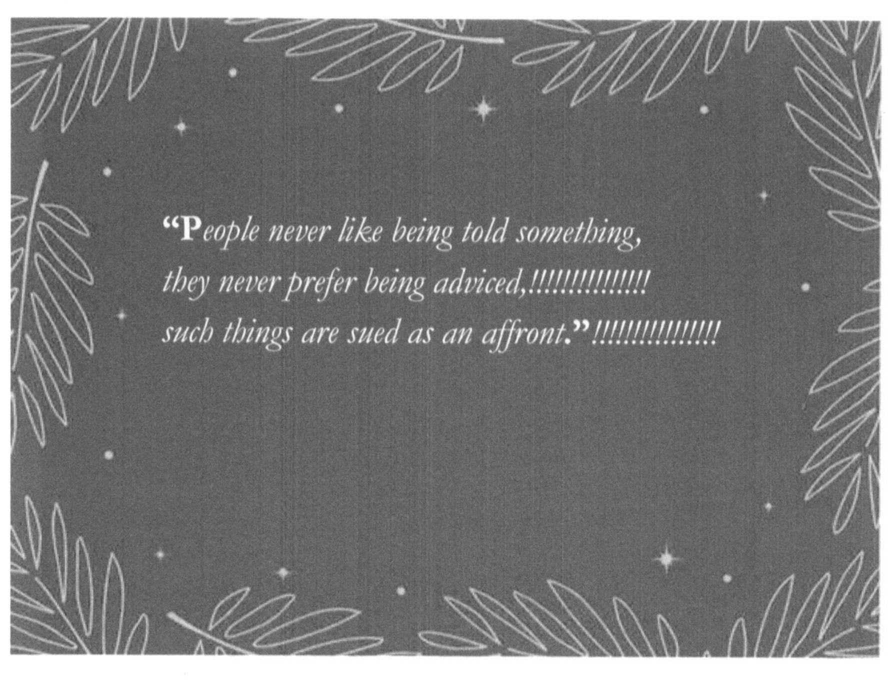

“For the majority of people around.........
people are just not aware of their goals in life........
For them it is a bit and run, or
A run and bit.”!!!!!!!!!!!!!!!!!!!!!!!!!!!!!!

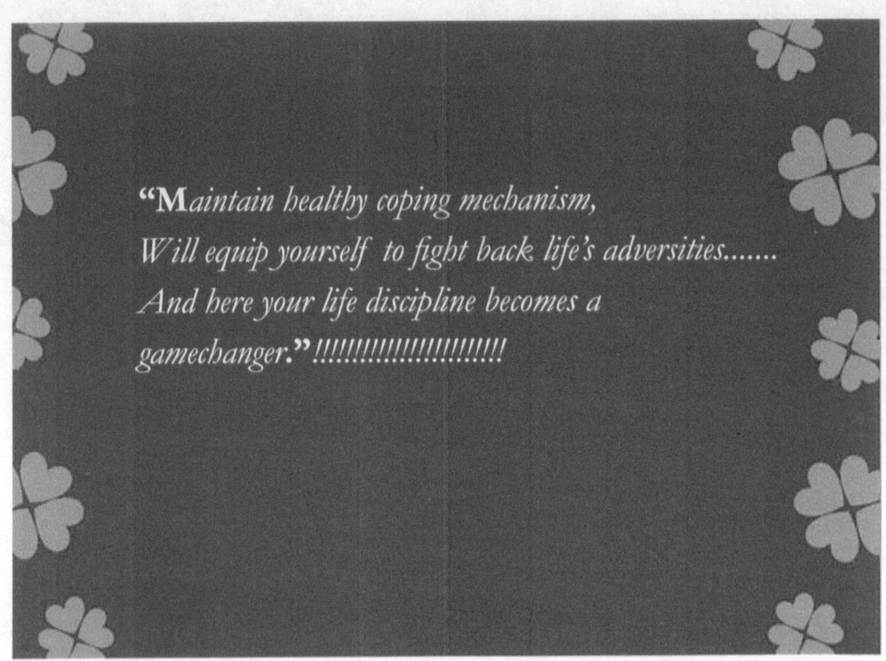

"Today a man is more involved in petty issues,
Than investing time for himself in becoming all that he wants to become,,,,,,,,,,,,,,,,
The social aura cheats him."!!!!!!!!!!!!!!!!!!!!!!!!!!!!!!!!!!!!!!

*"**Q**uiter people in our relationship,*
Are loosing their footage in our society,
Sufferance for them is intermittent."!!!!!!!!!!!!!!!!!!!!!!

*"**M**odern age man never admits his limitations,*
Rather he always puts a brave front, even knowing
Himself....
This behaviour definitively erodes his credibility."!!!!!!!!!!!

*"**I**n social spaces,*
People never apologise, even when they hurt others….
This tears relationships."!!

*"**I**n our social interactions, we often intrude into others Privacy..........................very casually*
Never ever pry into matters, that aren't meant for you,
For deep social cohesion."!!!!!!!!!!!!!!!!!!!!!!!!!!!!!!!!!!!!

*"**P**overty snatches innocence fast......*
Poverty thrusts responsibility too young,
Poverty makes you maturer fast!!!!!!!!!!
Poverty makes man wiser fast."!!!!!!!!!!!!!!!!!!!!!!!!!

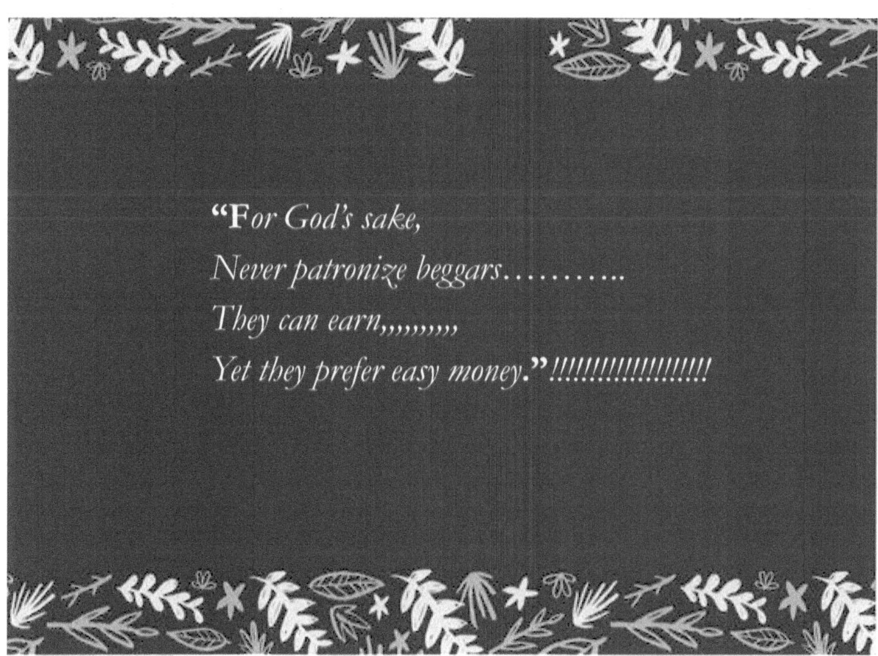

Education

*"**A**n educative man becomes,*
Behaviourally strong,
It also reinforces morality." !!!!!!!!!!!!!!!!!!!!!!!!!!!!

*"**N**ever overwhelm yourself with knowledge,*
It breeds arrogance......,..............
Be wise with your learning." !!!!!!!!!!!!!!!!!!!!!!!

*"**K**nowledge was never an end in itself,*
It is a means,
Sharing it with others, is it's worthwhile end." !!!!!!!!!!

*"**A**ll learning boils down to,...............*
Creating emotional stability,
Handling your stress, and
Solving problems amicably............
You are supposed to be finetuned in these gestures." !!!!!!!!!!!!!!!!!!!!!

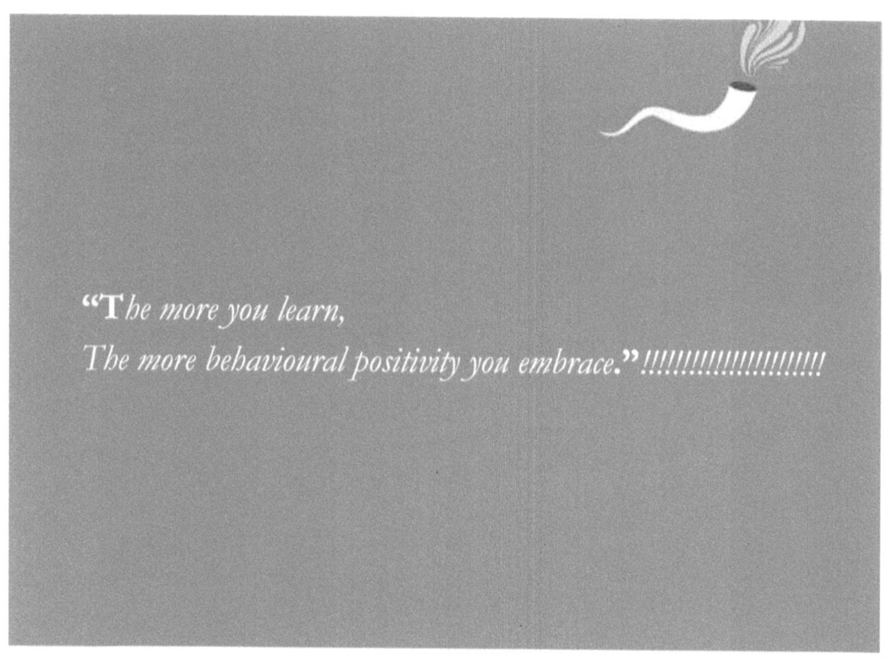

“**A** *good book helps you,*
Climb your perspective!!!!!!!!!!!!!!

*"**W**ith too much knowledge you become Behaviourally weak."*!!!!!!!!!!!!!!!!!!!!

*" '**B**e a student of life for life' as a quote goes, In man's life, learning never stops like breath."*!!!!!!!!!!!!!!!!!!!!!!!!!!!!!!!!

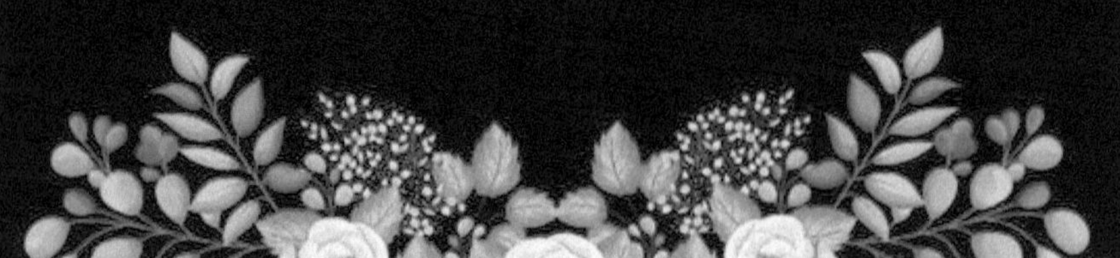

"**A** *head full of knowledge,*
Invariably forgets the head itself." !!!!!!!!!!!!!!!

"**U***nless you hone your mind,*
By regularly challenging it,
Your cognitive faculty will fade fast." !!!!!!!!!!!!!!!

"E*ducation makes you mellower..........*
It is just behavioural."!!!!!!!!!!!!!!!!!!!!!!!!!!!!

"W*ith books, we become......*
Playful, mindful, learnful
And above all sensuous."!!!!!!!!!!!!!!!!!!

"**T***he greatest role and value that education ought to inculcate,!!!!!!!!!!!!!!!!*
The capacity to distinguish between a right and a wrong......
A man brimming with righteousness, is foremostly educated."*!!!*

"**E***xcessive learning,*
Needs moderate unlearning too!!!!!!!!!!!!!
Decluttering of the mind is essential."*!!!!!!!!!!!!!*

*“**M**usic has,*
Lesser boundaries than language!!!!!!!!!!!!!!!!!!
It has a quietness of an inhale.” !!!!!!!!!!!!!!!!!!!!!!

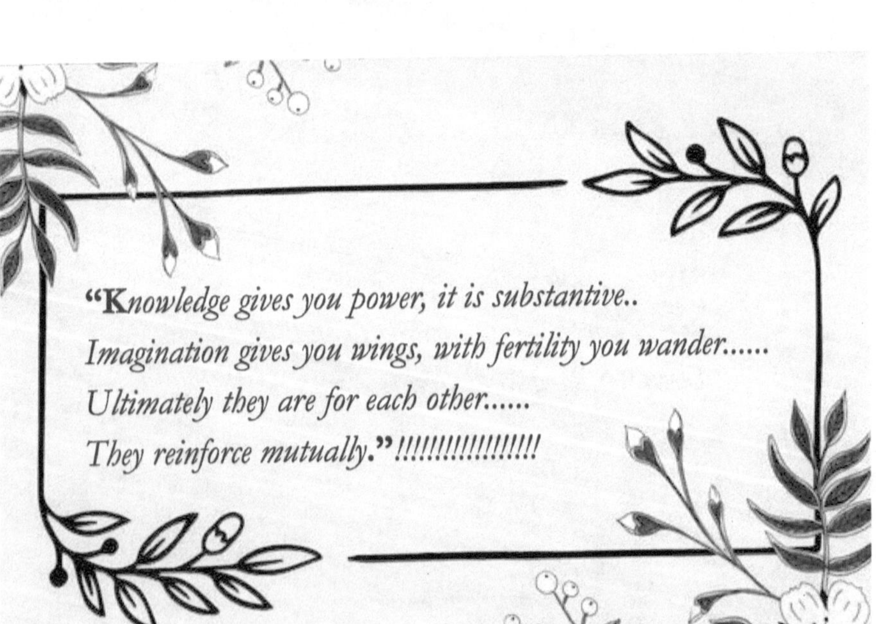

*"**K**nowledge tells us that every things is fine,*
Wisdom whispers that all is not well with the world."!!!!!!!!!!!!!!!!!!!!!!!!!

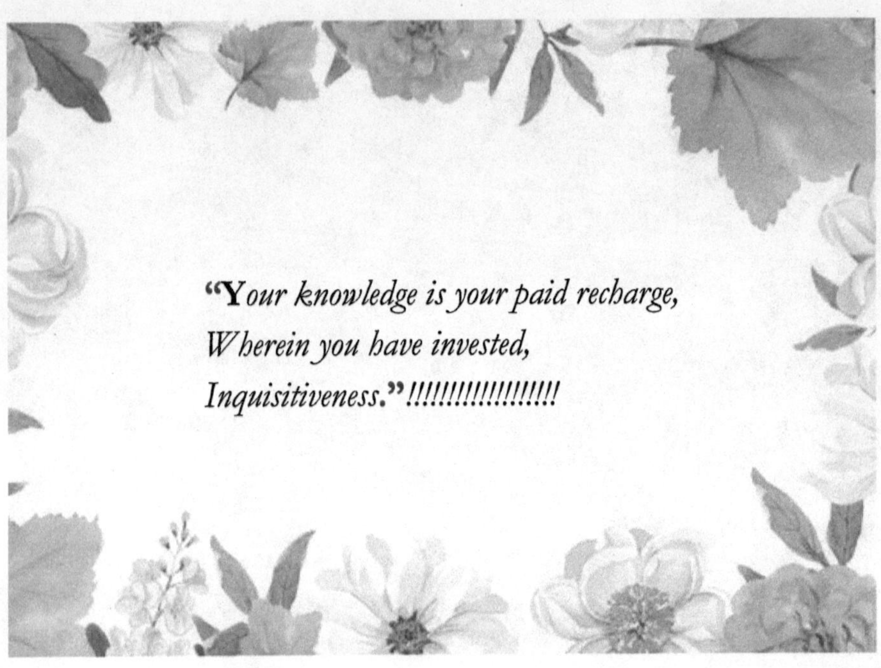

*"**Y**our knowledge is your paid recharge,*
Wherein you have invested,
Inquisitiveness." !!!!!!!!!!!!!!!!!!!

*"**E**ducation gives you a*
Valued behaviour." !!!!!!!!!!!!!!!!

"**W***ho are eating the Peace in society????*
The army of educated populace............
Whether it be........
Racism, Bigotry, Disparity, Attitudinal trajectory,
Too much education gives toxicity to the mind,
Simplicity is torn apart."!!!!!!!!!!!!!!!!!!!!!

"**E***ducation empowers...*
It sets you free,
It gives vision,
And allows you to sail off."!!!!!!!!!!!!!!!!!!!!!

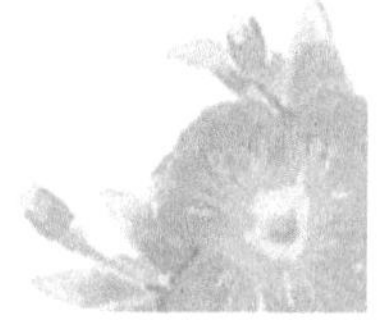

"Learning is Theft Free...............
It doesn't need a digilocker."!!!!!!!!!!!!!!!!!!!!!

"Listening is always more
Empowering than speaking
It educates."!!!!!!!!!!!!!!!!!!!!!!!!!

"True education,
Softens you, it mellows too." !!!!!!!!!!!!!!

"Learning was never meant for earning grades.....
Learning is always there for making man
Behaviorally enriched and morally disciplined." !!!!!!!!!!!

“Never stop learning,
For somewhere down the line,
Learning is a straight line that never rests,
Comforting is decaying.”!!!!!!!!!!!!!!!!!!!!!!!

“Even if, having no formal education,
A reflective mind is fully educated.”!!!!!!!!!!!!

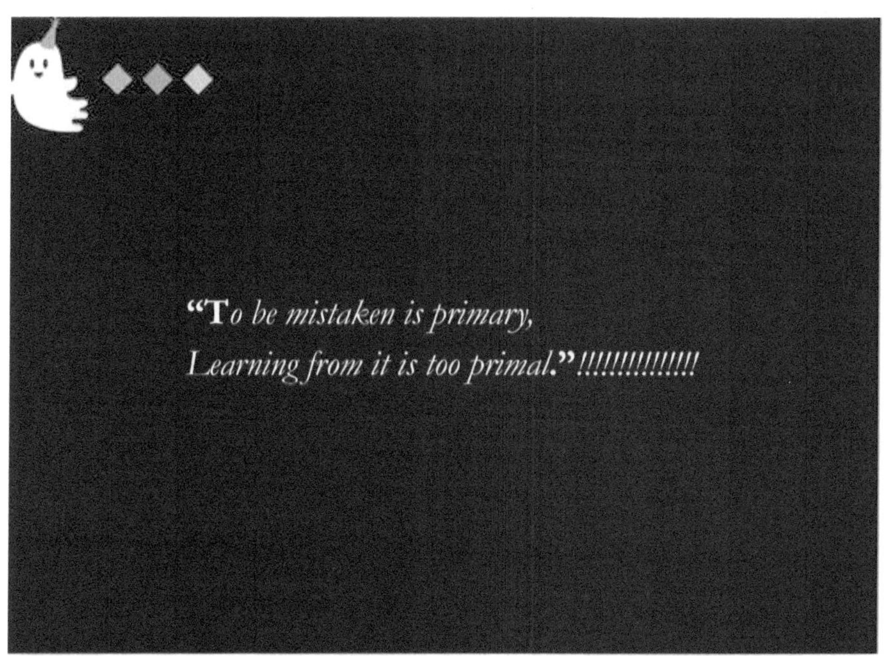

"To be mistaken is primary,
Learning from it is too primal." !!!!!!!!!!!!!!

"A good teacher must be honest in his credentials.......................
And teachers with high salaries never teach." !!!!!!!!!!

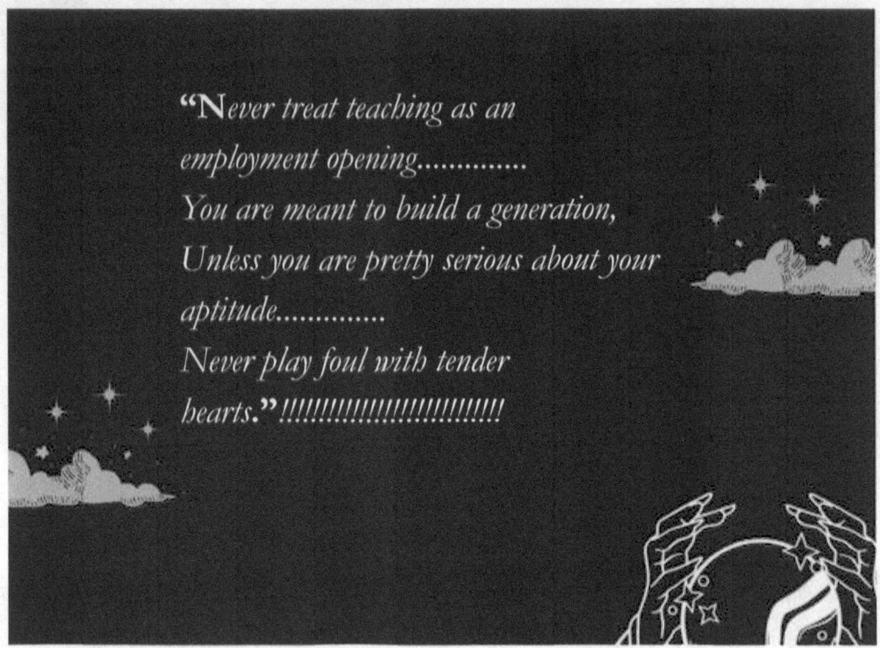
"Never treat teaching as an
employment opening.............
You are meant to build a generation,
Unless you are pretty serious about your
aptitude.............
Never play foul with tender
hearts." !!!!!!!!!!!!!!!!!!!!!!!!!!!!

"Memory is a spiders web,
Never trust............
A pen is mightier." !!!!!!!!!!!!!!!!!!!

"A *man who is wrapped up with Nature.........*
Has an education of the first order." *!!!!!!!!!!!!!!!!!!!!!*

Peace

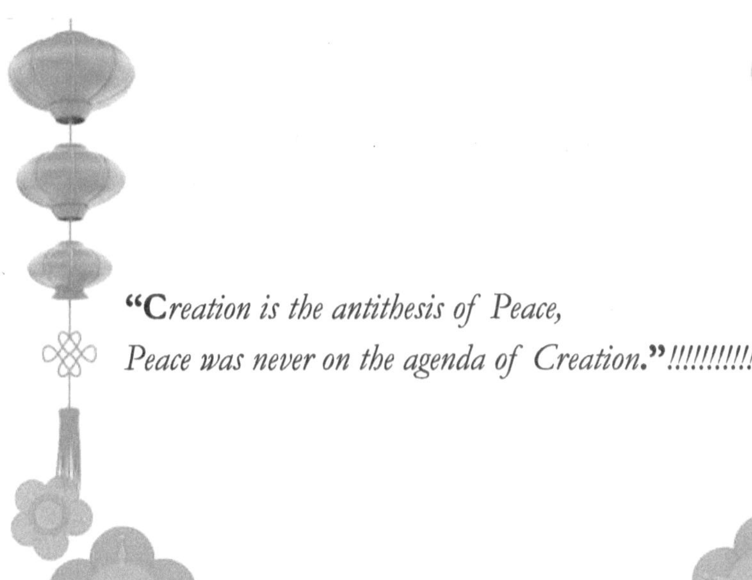

*"**C**reation is the antithesis of Peace,*
Peace was never on the agenda of Creation."!!!!!!!!!!!

*"**P**eace is not on earth,*
Heavens too are commotive and long for Peace,
And Hell is Hell."!!!!!!!!!!!!!!!!!!!!!!!!!!!!!!!!!!!!!!

*“**P**eace is a civilizational Enigma.”!!!!!!!!!!!!!!!!!!*

*“**W**ith all God Graces,*
Man was never born to reap the dividends of
‘Peace’.”!!!!!!!!!!!!!!!!!!!!!!!!!!

*"**W**hen you let go things, that are beyond your reach,*
You buy peace, an inner sense of ease...................
Always be for thing, within your reach."!!!!!!!!!!!!!!!!!

*"**Y**our "Peace" always comes from within,*
Don't ever search with floodlights in the jungle."!!!!!!!!!!!!

"**A***nything that brings peace and purpose,*
Is just worth everything."!!!!!!!!!!!!!!!!!!!!!!!!!

"**I***f history is to be seen,*
For a solution to bringing Peace,
War is the worst option."!!!!!!!!!!!!!!!

"T*he tragedy with man is,*
He never finds peace within................
He chases it ...above, below, underneath,
*beneath.***"** *!!!!!!!!!!!!!!!!*

"B*uy Peace,*
Purchase Peace,
Run for it,!!!!!!!!!!!!!!!
*For your mind is in dire need of it.***"** *!!!!!!!!!!!!!!*

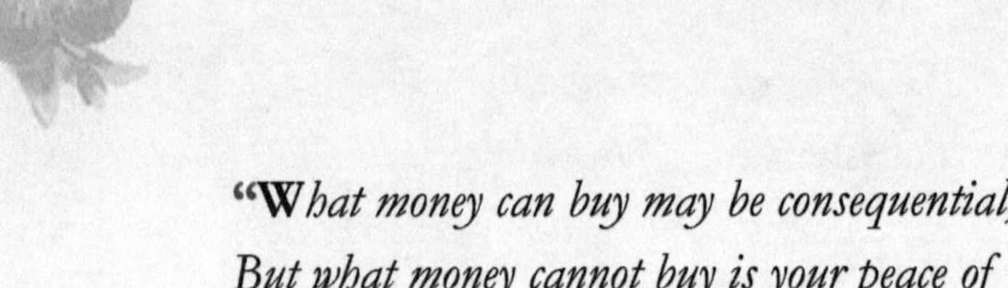

"What money can buy may be consequential,
But what money cannot buy is your peace of mind." !!!!!!!!!!!!!!!!!!!!

"Peace in our times,
Is demanding Justice." !!!!!!!!!!!!!!

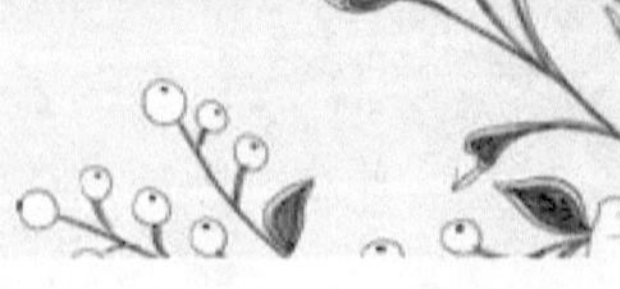

"**F***orgiveness brings, With it,*
An empowering Peace."*!!!!!!!!!!*

"**P***eace emanates,*
It is not Taught."*!!!!!!!!!!!!*

"I*f anywhere you learn that Peace is being auctioned*
Then give it your highest bid to procure it
Even to the limit of your sellout
Peace is the most valuable asset
On earth."*!!*

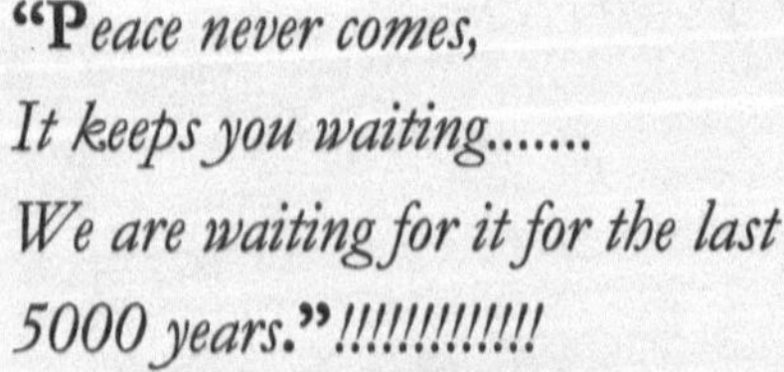

"P*eace never comes,*
It keeps you waiting.......
We are waiting for it for the last
5000 years."*!!!!!!!!!!!!!*

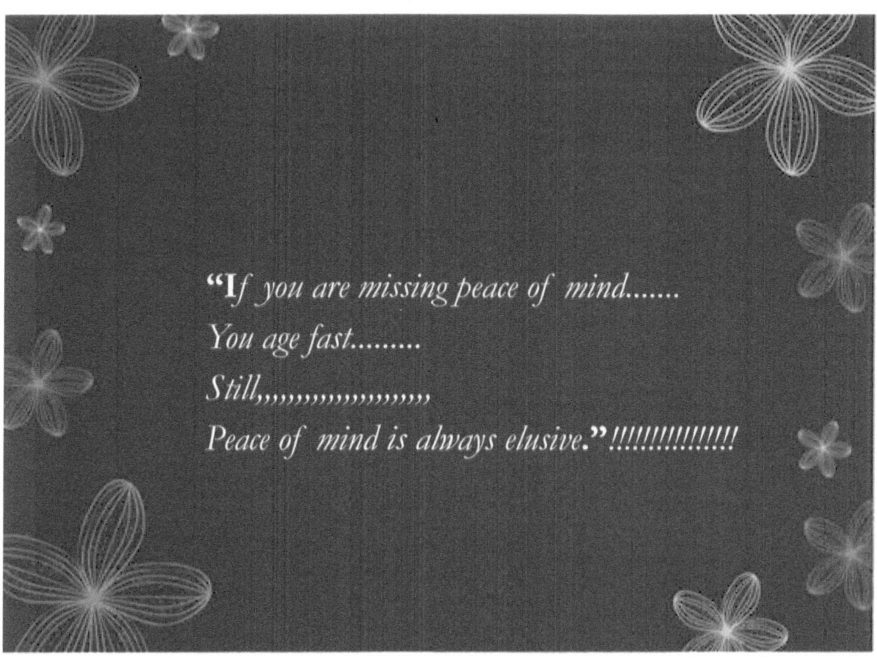

"If you are missing peace of mind.......
You age fast.........
Still,,,,,,,,,,,,,,,,,,,,,,,
Peace of mind is always elusive."!!!!!!!!!!!!!!!

Truth

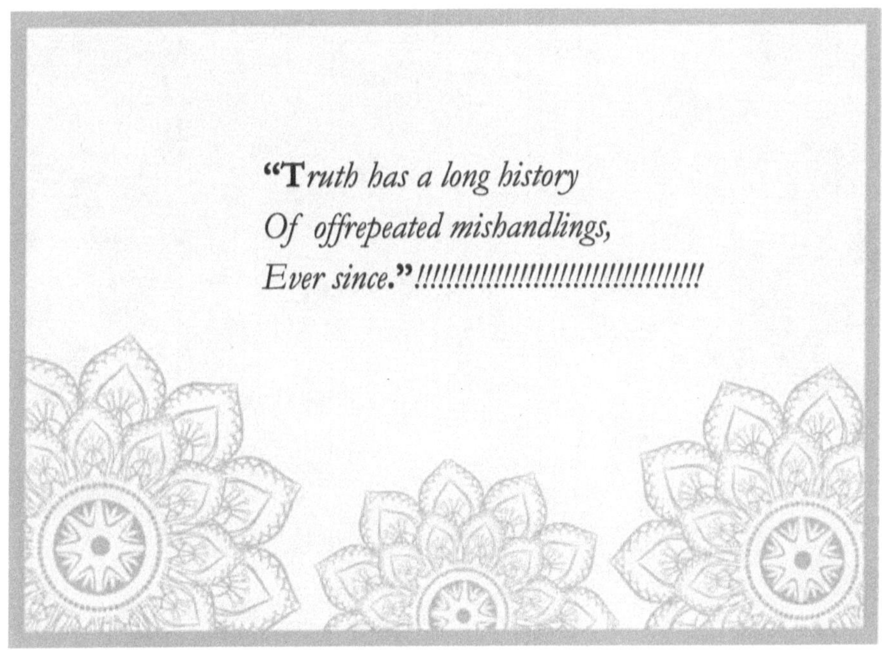
"T*ruth has a long history*
Of offrepeated mishandlings,
Ever since."!!!!!!!!!!!!!!!!!!!!!!!!!!!!!!!!!!!!

"T*ruth has multiple shade,*
Lie too is multiple shaded,
Man is not made to reach them out."!!!!!!!!!!!!!

*“**R**ight and wrong are plural,*
Both have multiple truths.”!!!!!!!!!!!!

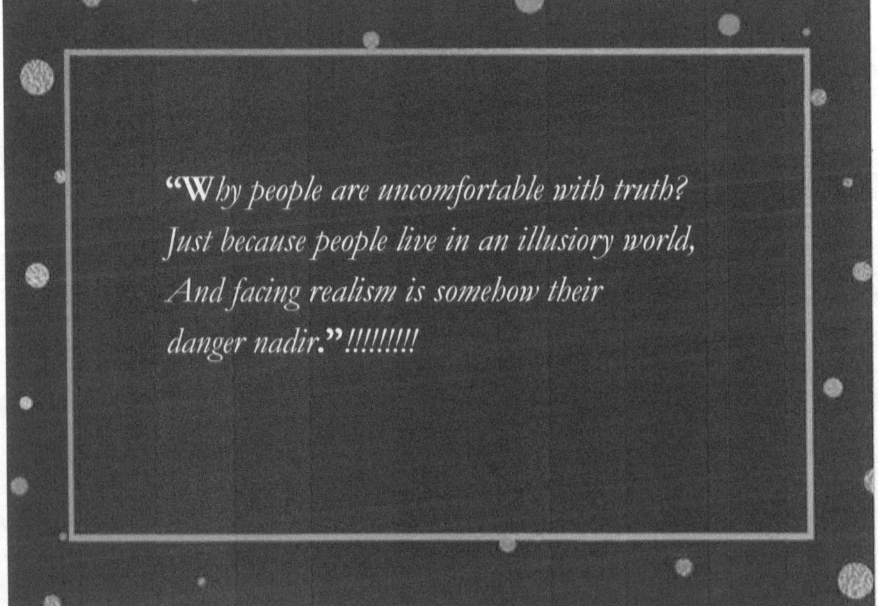

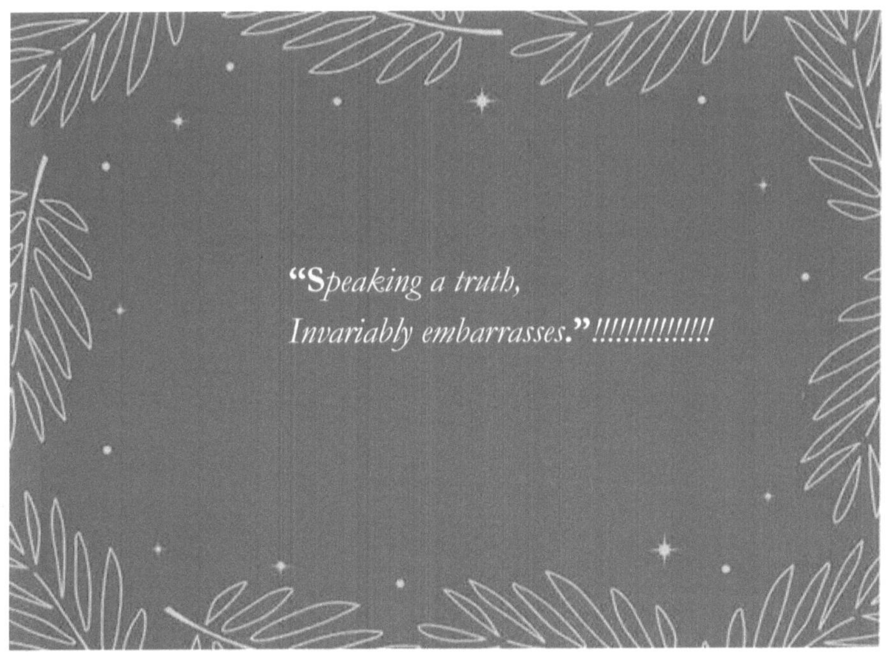

"The world fears truth speakers............
For they make things running on their heads."!!!!!!!!!!!!!!!!!!!!

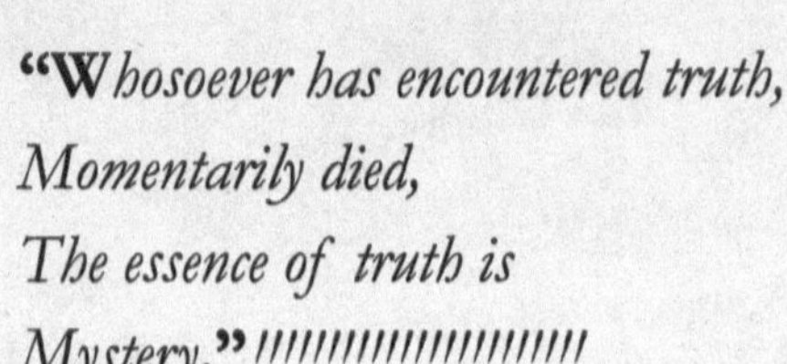

“**W***hosoever has encountered truth,*
Momentarily died,
The essence of truth is
Mystery.” *!!!!!!!!!!!!!!!!!!!!!!!*

“**T***ruth mystifies.*” *!!!!!!!!!!!!!!!!!!!!!!!!*

"People who know the truth,
Are in the habit of shutting up their mouth."!!!!!!!!!!!!!!

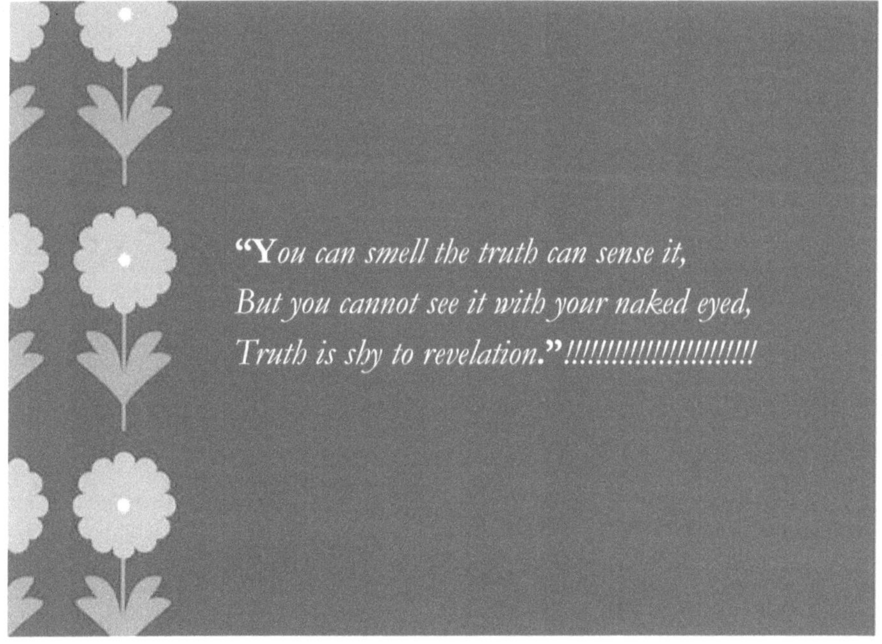
"You can smell the truth can sense it,
But you cannot see it with your naked eyed,
Truth is shy to revelation."!!!!!!!!!!!!!!!!!!!!!!!!

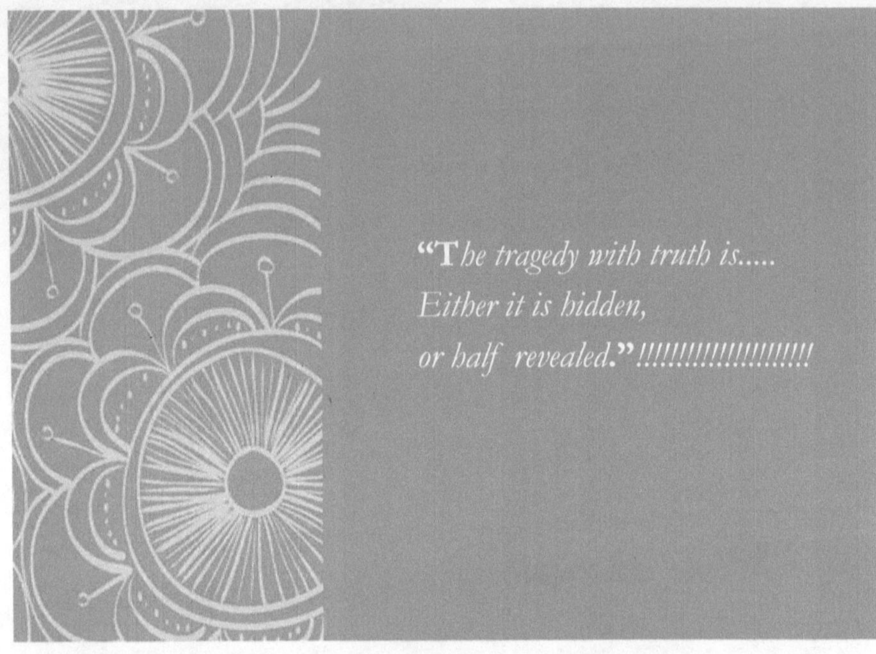
"The tragedy with truth is.....
Either it is hidden,
or half revealed."!!!!!!!!!!!!!!!!!!!!!

"Once you are true to Yourself
You never need any other Truth."!!!!!!!!!!!

*“**T**he only expression that goes in,*
Making you simplest........
Is speak the truth.”!!!!!!!!!!!!!!!!!!!!!!!!!!

*“**T**ruth has a Feel, It also smells....*
But you have to be intuitive,
To discover, Its wholeness.”!!!!!!!!!!!!!!!!!!!!!!!!!!!!!!!!!

"Wisdom always co-partners truthfulness."!!!!!!!!!!

www.ingramcontent.com/pod-product-compliance
Lightning Source LLC
LaVergne TN
LVHW091257150826
845673LV00006B/1453

9798896107262